People, Places, and Things 1

Reading · Vocabulary · Test Preparation

Lin Lougheed

OXFORD
UNIVERSITY PRESS

OXFORD
UNIVERSITY PRESS

198 Madison Avenue
New York, NY 10016 USA

Great Clarendon Street, Oxford OX2 6DP UK

Oxford University Press is a department of the University of Oxford.
It furthers the University's objective of excellence in research, scholarship,
and education by publishing worldwide in

Oxford New York

Auckland Cape Town Dar es Salaam Hong Kong Karachi
Kuala Lumpur Madrid Melbourne Mexico City Nairobi
New Delhi Shanghai Taipei Toronto

With offices in

Argentina Austria Brazil Chile Czech Republic France Greece
Guatemala Hungary Italy Japan Poland Portugal Singapore
South Korea Switzerland Thailand Turkey Ukraine Vietnam

OXFORD and OXFORD ENGLISH are registered trademarks of
Oxford University Press

Library of Congress Cataloging-in-Publication Data

Lougheed, Lin, 1946–
    People, places, and things : reading, vocabulary, test preparation / Lin Lougheed.
       p. cm.
    Includes indexes.
    ISBN-13: 978-0-19-430200-5 (student bk. : level 1)
    ISBN-10: 0-19-430200-8 (student bk. : level 1)
[etc.]
    1. English language—Textbooks for foreign speakers. 2. English language—Examinations—
Study guides. I. Title.

PE1128.L648 2005
428'.0076—dc22   2005049800

Executive Publisher: Nancy Leonhardt
Senior Acquisitions Editor: Chris Balderston
Editor: Anna Teevan
Assistant Editor: Kate Schubert
Art Director: Maj-Britt Hagsted
Senior Designer: Mia Gomez
Production Manager: Shanta Persaud
Production Controller: Eve Wong

Additional realia by Mia Gomez

ISBN-13: 978 0 19 430200 5
ISBN-10: 0 19 430200 8

10 9 8 7 6 5 4 3 2 1

Printed in Hong Kong.

Acknowledgments:

Cover photographs: Lee Young-Pyo: AP Photo/Hussein Malla; Mount Lhotse and Mount Everest:
©Brad Wrobleski/Masterfile; Stonehenge: ©SuperStock/Alamy; Chinese Dragon:
©ImageState/Alamy; Tropical fish: ©ImageState/Alamy; Midori Ito: ©Neal Preston/CORBIS.

We would like to thank the following for their permission to reproduce photographs:
AP Photo/Gorilla Foundation p.12; AP Photo/Wally Santana p.54; ©Michel Arnaud/CORBIS p.42;
Stephen Chernin/Getty Images p.6; Ron Cohn/Gorilla Foundation p.16; ©Tim Davis/CORBIS pp.24,
66; ©Everett Collection p.32; Romeo Gacad/AFP/Getty Images p.74; The Granger Collection, New
York p.62; ©Randall Hyman p.46; Christian Kaiser/laif p.14; ©Viviane Moos/CORBIS p.36; ©Josef
Polleross/CORBIS p.26; ©Neal Preston/CORBIS p.72; ©Rick Rickman/NewSport/CORBIS p.76; ©Joel
W. Rogers/CORBIS p.56; Hugh Sitton p.34; Tim Sloan/AFP/Getty Images p.2; ©Paul A. Souders/COR-
BIS p.64; ©Alexander Stewart p.22; TAIPEI 101/AFP/Getty Images p.52; ©Betsie Van der Meer p.44;
©Warner Bros/Everett Collection p.4.

CONTENTS

TO THE TEACHER

Welcome to *People, Places, and Things*.

What is in each unit?

Prepare to Read
This section introduces the topic of the passage. The questions encourage students to share their own thoughts and experiences, and can be used for discussion before reading.

Word Focus
This matching activity introduces students to new or unfamiliar words that they will see in the reading passage. Students match the ten words with simple definitions.

Scan
This activity encourages students to make a prediction about a specific piece of information that appears in the passage. The aim is to motivate students to read the passages quickly as they try to find the answer.

Reading Passage
Each reading passage in Book 1 is about 150 words. The eight units each contain three reading passages based around a common theme: the first passage is about a person, the second is about a place, and the third is about a thing. Each reading passage recycles new words from earlier passages so that students can gradually build on and consolidate their vocabulary. The language is carefully graded so that students gain confidence in reading. Each reading passage is also available on an audio CD, narrated by a native English speaker. The CD is available separately.

Which Meaning?
This feature focuses on a word in the passage that has more than one dictionary meaning. Students must choose which of the dictionary definitions fits the word as it is used in the context of the passage. The aim is to encourage students to use dictionaries more effectively, and to think about the meaning of words in context.

Check Your Comprehension
These multiple-choice questions check students' understanding of the passage. The questions include key skills such as understanding the main idea, reading for details, reading for inference, and understanding text references.

Vocabulary Review
This section reviews the vocabulary presented in the unit. It includes a wide variety of activities, such as Words in Context (filling in the gaps), Sentence Completion (completing short advertisements and e-mails), and Wrong Word (finding the word that doesn't fit the group). Other activities include Word Families, Synonyms and Antonyms, True or False, and puzzles such as Crosswords, Word Searches, and Mystery Phrases. The aim is to help students begin to use the new words as part of their active vocabulary.

What About You?

This section is divided into two parts: Speaking and Writing. The aim is to encourage students to use some of the new words they have learned in a more personal context. The activity can be done in pairs or in small groups.

Reading Quiz

This features a short passage—an e-mail, a letter or a short information piece—followed by six multiple choice test questions. The passage includes many of the new words from the unit. The multiple choice format and the range of question types reflect the style of questions that students will encounter in standardized tests such as the TOIEC® and TOEFL® tests. The aim of the quiz is to act as a unit test, and also to help students with test preparation.

Extra Features

Vocabulary Self-Quiz

This is a unit-by-unit word list which lists the new words in each passage. There is a space next to each word where students can write a translation, or other notes, and there is also a space for them to test themselves. The aim is to help students study and review the words outside class.

Vocabulary Index

This is an index of the new vocabulary items which appear in the passages. Each item is followed by a reference to the passage where it is introduced, and also to the subsequent passages where it reappears.

Answer Key

The Answer Key is available on the OUP Website, and can be downloaded at www.oup.com/elt/teacher/peopleplacesandthings.

ACKNOWLEDGMENTS

The author and publisher would like to thank the following teachers, whose reviews, comments, and suggestions contributed to the development of *People, Places, and Things*:

Jeong Mi Choi, BCM Junior High School, Seoul, Korea; Jeremy Greenway, Shinmin Senior High School, Taichung, Taiwan; Sabrina Hsieh, Sacred Heart High School, Touliu, Taiwan; Shigeru Ichikawa, Todaiji Gakuen Junior and Senior High Schools, Nara, Japan; Tae Woo Kang, Kang Tae Woo Language School, Seoul, Korea; Josie Lai, Hsin Sheng Children's English School, Taoyuan, Taiwan; Jessie Lee, Tunghai University, Taichung, Taiwan; Masahiro Shirai, Doshisha Girls' Junior and Senior High Schools, Kyoto, Japan; Atsuko Tsuda, Keio Gijuku University, Tokyo, Japan; Arthur Tu, Taipei YMCA, Taipei, Taiwan.

In addition, the author would like to thank the following for their helpful comments and suggestions: Richard Firsten, Lindsey Hopkins Technical Education Center, Miami, Florida, U.S.A.; Maureen McCarthy, Miami Dade College, Miami, Florida, U.S.A.; Christine Meloni, Ph.D., George Washington University, Washington, DC, U.S.A.; Maureen O'Hara, Miami Dade College, Miami, Florida, U.S.A.; Katherine Rawson, Montgomery College, Montgomery County, Maryland U.S.A.; Cynthia Schuemann, Miami Dade College, Miami, Florida, U.S.A.

HARRY POTTER

PEOPLE

J.K. Rowling

PREPARE TO READ
Discuss these questions.

1. Who is your favorite writer?

2. What do you know about J.K. Rowling?

WORD FOCUS
Match the words with their definitions.

A.
1. author __   **a.** a writer
2. continue __   **b.** the time when you finish school
3. famous __   **c.** become an adult
4. graduation __   **d.** not stop; keep going
5. grow up __   **e.** describes a person that everybody knows

B.
1. make up __   **a.** someone who makes books
2. passion __   **b.** think of (a new idea)
3. publisher __   **c.** write on paper
4. rabbit __   **d.** love for something or someone
5. write down __   **e.** a small animal with long ears

SCAN
A. Guess if this is true or false. Circle *a* or *b*.
J.K. Rowling studied English at university.

a. True   *b.* False

B. Scan the passage quickly to check your answer.

J.K. Rowling

Do you **make up** stories for your friends and family? Do you **write** these stories **down**? J.K. Rowling did. She had a **passion** to tell stories. She loved to write. Now she's a **famous author**.

When Joanna Rowling was young, she was like other children. She went to
5 school, did her homework, and played with her friends. But Rowling also made up stories for her sister. These stories were usually about **rabbits** because they both liked rabbits. As she **grew up**, she **continued** writing stories about her friends in school.

Rowling wrote all the time. At the university she studied French, but she still
10 wrote stories. After **graduation** she taught English in Portugal. There she continued to work on a story about a boy. She decided to <u>call</u> him Harry Potter. Later, she went to Scotland and worked as a French teacher. She finally finished her book there. It took another year to find a **publisher**.

Rowling never stopped doing what she wanted
15 to do. It took her six years to write the first Harry Potter book, but she never stopped writing. Now we can all read her stories and share her passion.

WHICH MEANING?
What does *call* mean in line 11?
1 (*verb*) to phone a person
2 (*verb*) to give someone a name
3 (*noun*) a phone conversation

CHECK YOUR COMPREHENSION

Read the passage again and answer the questions. Circle your answers.

MAIN IDEA

1. What is this reading mainly about?

A. Harry Potter

B. A story writer

C. A new book

D. J.K. Rowling's jobs

DETAIL

2. Before she became a famous author, what did Rowling do?

A. She worked for a publisher.

B. She played with rabbits.

C. She was a teacher.

D. She lived with a French family.

3. Why did Rowling go to Portugal?

A. To publish stories

B. To read books

C. To teach English

D. To learn French

4. What were Rowling's first stories about?

A. Rabbits

B. Portugal

C. Harry Potter

D. Teaching

5. Where did Rowling teach French?

A. In Scotland

B. In France

C. In Portugal

D. In England

INFERENCE

6. What is true about Rowling?

A. She taught Portuguese.

B. She worked in France.

C. She was always writing.

D. She never played with her sister.

PLACES

PREPARE TO READ
Discuss these questions.

1. What is your favorite subject in school?

2. Look at the children in the picture. What do you think they study in school?

WORD FOCUS
Match the words with their definitions.

A.

1. castle __
2. magic __
3. ordinary __
4. recess __
5. broom __

a. special power
b. We use this to clean the floor.
c. a big, old, stone building
d. the time to play at school
e. usual; normal

B.

1. witch __
2. wizard __
3. invisible __
4. attend __
5. monster __

a. a big, frightening person in a story
b. go to
c. a girl or woman who does magic
d. You can't see it.
e. a boy or man who does magic

SCAN
A. Guess the answer. Circle *a* or *b*.

What is the name of Harry Potter's School?

a. Hogwarts   *b.* Castle School

B. Scan the passage quickly to check your answer.

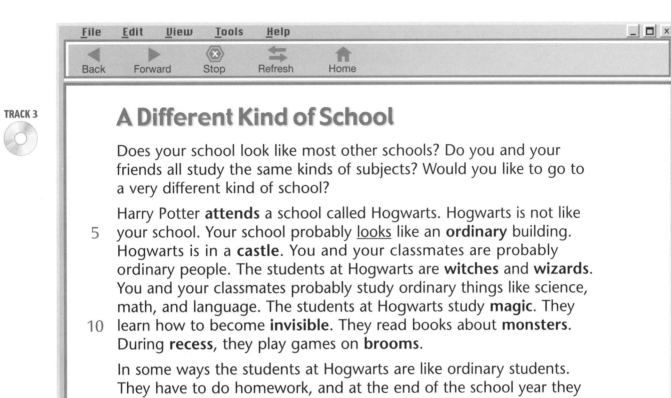

A Different Kind of School

Does your school look like most other schools? Do you and your friends all study the same kinds of subjects? Would you like to go to a very different kind of school?

Harry Potter **attends** a school called Hogwarts. Hogwarts is not like
5   your school. Your school probably <u>looks</u> like an **ordinary** building. Hogwarts is in a **castle**. You and your classmates are probably ordinary people. The students at Hogwarts are **witches** and **wizards**. You and your classmates probably study ordinary things like science, math, and language. The students at Hogwarts study **magic**. They
10   learn how to become **invisible**. They read books about **monsters**. During **recess**, they play games on **brooms**.

In some ways the students at Hogwarts are like ordinary students. They have to do homework, and at the end of the school year they have to take exams. Hogwarts is not an
15   ordinary school, but it is still a school.

WHICH MEANING?
What does *looks* mean in line 5?
1 (*noun*) the appearance of something
2 (*verb*) seems to be
3 (*verb*) uses one's eyes

CHECK YOUR COMPREHENSION

Read the passage again and answer the questions. Circle your answers.

MAIN IDEA

1. What is the main topic of this passage?

  A. Types of magic
  B. Harry Potter's school
  C. Homework and exams
  D. Harry Potter's friends

DETAIL

2. What is Hogwarts?

  A. A school for ordinary children
  B. An invisible school
  C. A school for witches and wizards
  D. A math school

3. What do the students at Hogwarts study?

  A. Language
  B. Science
  C. Monsters
  D. Castles

4. What do the students at Hogwarts do during recess?

  A. They play on brooms.
  B. They clean the floor.
  C. They read books.
  D. They do their homework.

5. What makes the students at Hogwarts special?

  A. They always study math.
  B. They can make themselves invisible.
  C. They speak many languages.
  D. They play with monsters.

INFERENCE

6. At the end of the school year, what do Hogwarts students do?

  A. Buy new brooms
  B. Clean the castle
  C. Study for their exams
  D. Learn new games

PREPARE TO READ

Discuss these questions.

1. What are some movies that are also books?

2. What things do you have that are related to movies or books?

WORD FOCUS

Match the words with their definitions.

A.

1. event __   **a.** 1,000,000
2. available __   **b.** people in stories
3. million __   **c.** You can get it.
4. costumes __   **d.** something special that happens
5. characters __   **e.** special clothes

B.

1. imagine __   **a.** places to find information on the Internet
2. Websites __   **b.** have a picture of something in your mind
3. series __   **c.** a set of things, like books
4. put on __   **d.** things that are made
5. products __   **e.** take and wear clothes

SCAN

A. Guess if this is true or false. Circle *a* or *b*.

Bookstores have sold over 250 million Harry Potter books.

a. True   *b.* False

B. Scan the passage quickly to check your answer.

The Business of Harry Potter

The first book of the seven-book Harry Potter **series** came to the bookstores in 1997. Since then, bookstores have sold more than 250 **million** copies of the
5 first books in the series. These books are **available** in more than 200 countries and in more than 60 languages.

When a new Harry Potter book arrives in the bookstores, it is always a big
10 **event**. Usually, the first books are sold at the magic hour of midnight. Stores that usually close at 6:00 P.M. stay open late for the special event. People wait in <u>line</u> for hours, sometimes days, to buy
15 a book. Many children and even some adults **put on costumes** to look like their favorite **characters** in the book.

Harry Potter is more than a book series. It is a very large business. You can see
20 Harry Potter movies. You can buy Harry Potter **products** like DVDs, videos, dolls, costumes, pictures, games, and toys–almost anything you can **imagine**, even fast food. There are also Harry
25 Potter **Websites**. These Websites give information about Harry and his friends as well as sell Harry Potter products. Thanks to the business of Harry Potter, J.K. Rowling is one of the richest
30 women in the world. She is richer than the Queen of England.

WHICH MEANING?
What does *line* mean in line 14?
1 (*noun*) a row of people
2 (*verb*) to cover the inside of something
3 (*noun*) a mark on a piece of paper

CHECK YOUR COMPREHENSION

Read the passage again and answer the questions. Circle your answers.

MAIN IDEA

1. What is this reading mainly about?
   A. Long lines
   B. Interesting costumes
   C. Bookstores
   D. Money and Harry Potter

DETAIL

2. Why do people wait in line for hours?
   A. To meet Harry Potter
   B. To look at costumes
   C. To buy a new Harry Potter book
   D. To get a free doll

3. In how many countries can you buy Harry Potter books?
   A. 7
   B. 60
   C. Over 200
   D. 1997

4. At what time are the first books sold?
   A. When the stores open
   B. At 6:00 P.M.
   C. Before midnight
   D. At midnight

INFERENCE

5. Which best describes the series?
   A. Many people like it.
   B. It is very expensive.
   C. People read it very quickly.
   D. None of the above

TEXT REFERENCE

6. In line 19, *It is a very large business*, what does the word *It* refer to?
   A. Costumes
   B. Books
   C. Harry Potter
   D. Characters

VOCABULARY REVIEW

CROSSWORD PUZZLE
Complete the crossword using the clues.

Across

2. If everybody knows you, you are _____.

3. Someone or a company that makes books.

5. She can do magic.

6. A feeling of love for something.

7. If you can't see something, it is _____.

Down

1. It has long ears and a short tail.

4. Things that people make to sell.

5. This is part of the Internet.

8. This cleans the floor.

WRONG WORD
One word in each group does not fit. Circle the word.

1. child	baby	rabbit	adult
2. witch	magic	wizard	ordinary
3. castle	house	building	broom
4. rabbit	monster	dog	mouse
5. series	ten	hundred	million
6. put on	write down	costume	clothes

WORDS IN CONTEXT
Fill in the blanks with words from each box.

available	continue	make up	attends	author

1. The books aren't in the bookstores now. They'll be _____ next week.

2. J.K. Rowling is the _____ of the Harry Potter series.

3. Harry Potter _____ a school called Hogwarts.

4. You did well in your English class this year. You should _____ studying English next year.

5. I like to _____ stories and tell them to my friends.

magic	line	imagine	event	costume

6. I'm going to dress like a wizard for the party. I'll put on my _____ when I get home.

7. I won first prize in the costume contest. It was a big _____ in my life.

8. Try to _____ what a school for wizards is like.

9. That man pulled a rabbit out of a hat. It was _____ .

10. There were a lot of people at the movie. We had to wait in _____ to buy tickets.

recess	products	ordinary	series	monsters

11. Put on your best clothes for the big event. Don't wear _____ clothes.

12. There are several books in the Harry Potter _____. I have three of them.

13. You can buy lots of different Harry Potter _____—from dolls to fast food!

14. The children play games at _____ before they return to their classes.

15. My little brother doesn't like to be alone at night. He's afraid of _____.

WORD FAMILIES
Fill in the blanks with words from each box.

attendance (*noun*)	attend (*verb*)	attentive (*adjective*)

1. My _____ is perfect. I never miss school.

2. I _____ an ordinary school. Harry Potter goes to a school for magic.

imagine (*verb*)	imagination (*noun*)	imaginative (*adjective*)

3. Writers like J.K. Rowling have a great _____.

4. Try to _____ yourself as one of the richest people in the world.

graduate (*noun*)	graduation (*noun*)	graduate (*verb*)

5. I am almost ready to finish school. I'll _____ next year.

6. I will have a big party for my _____.

PHRASAL VERBS
Circle the correct words.

1. Please *put / put on* your coat in the closet.

2. I'll *put / put on* my coat because it's very cold today.

3. Maya *put / put on* her books on your desk.

4. I'm a storyteller. I love to *make / make up* stories.

5. I don't want to play this game. Let's *make / make up* a new game.

6. Are you hungry? I can *make / make up* a sandwich for you.

7. This is a pretty town. It's a nice place for children to *grow / grow up*.

8. Bob has a beautiful garden. He *grew / grew up* a lot of nice flowers there.

9. When I *grow / grow up*, I want to have a good job and make a lot of money.

WHAT ABOUT YOU?
Speaking
Ask your partner these questions.

1. What do you call your mother and father?

2. What will you do when you grow up?

3. What clothes do you put on for school or work?

4. What Websites do you visit?

5. Who is your favorite story character?

Writing
Now write about your partner. Use your partner's answers to the questions.
Example: <u>Jin-Sung calls his mother Mom</u>.

1. _____

2. _____

3. _____

4. _____

5. _____

Read the passage and answer the questions. Circle your answers.

First, have these things available: two pieces of paper, a pencil, and an ordinary envelope.

5 Think of today's date. Multiply the year by two (for example, 2007 x 2 = 4014). Write this number on a piece of paper and put it in the envelope.

Now, put on your magician's hat.
10 It's show time! Give someone a piece of paper and a pencil and ask, "Write down the year you were born." Tell the person not to make up the numbers. All the
15 numbers must be true.

Next say, "Think of an important event in your life" (for example, the year the person started school). Say, "Write down the
20 year it happened."

Then say, "Write down the age you will be on December 31st this year."

Next ask, "How many years ago
25 was the important event? Write down that number."

Ask the person to add the four numbers. Ask, "What is the total?" Open your envelope.
30 The numbers will be the same.

That's magic!

MAIN IDEA

1. What kind of passage is this?

A. An advertisement

B. A story

C. A list of instructions

D. An article

2. What is this passage mainly about?

A. Things to do with paper and pencil

B. How to add numbers

C. How to do a magic trick

D. Important events in life

DETAIL

3. What number will the magician start with?

A. The year of an important event

B. A birth date

C. Someone's age

D. Today's date

4. What is the total of the four numbers?

A. The year the person was born

B. The number in the envelope

C. Twice the person's age

D. Half today's date

TEXT REFERENCE

5. In line 26, *Write down that number*, what does the word *that* refer to?

A. Your birth date

B. Your age

C. Years since an important event

D. The year of an important event

VOCABULARY

6. What does *ordinary* in line 3 mean?

A. Available

B. Favorite

C. Invisible

D. Not special

UNIT 2 GORILLAS

PEOPLE

Dr. Francine Patterson

PREPARE TO READ
Discuss these questions.
1. What kinds of animals do you like? Why?
2. Look at the photo. What is Dr. Patterson's job?

WORD FOCUS
Match the words with their definitions.

A.
1. communicate __   a. a person
2. fireworks __   b. a short or special name
3. human __   c. talk
4. gorilla __   d. colored fire in the sky
5. nickname __   e. a large animal from Africa that looks
                          like a hairy person

B.
1. psychology __   a. a park for animals
2. research __   b. looking for information
3. feel __   c. the study of how people think
4. sign language __   d. be happy, sad, afraid, etc.
5. zoo __   e. a way of talking with the hands,
                          not the mouth

SCAN
A. Guess the answer. Circle *a* or *b*.
Dr. Patterson's student, Koko, is

a. a child.   *b.* a gorilla.

B. Scan the passage quickly to check your answer.

Dr. Francine Patterson

Most teachers don't teach the same student for longer than one year, but Dr. Francine Patterson has taught one student for <u>over</u> thirty years. Her student, Koko, is not an ordinary student. Koko is a **gorilla**.

5 In 1972, Francine Patterson was a student, too. She attended Stanford University in California and did **research** in **psychology**. As part of her research, she worked with a one-year-old gorilla at the San Francisco **Zoo**. The gorilla's name is Hanabi-Ko. This means "child of **fireworks**" in Japanese. Her nickname is Koko. Francine
10 Patterson has a **nickname**, too. It's Penny.

Penny taught Koko to **communicate** with **sign language**. Penny learned a lot from Koko, who had a lot to say. She learned that gorillas can think, imagine, and **feel**; and that gorillas, like **humans**, can communicate their thoughts and feelings.

15 Penny and Koko are now famous. Penny is a published author, and Koko has her own Website.

WHICH MEANING?
What does *over* mean in line 2?

1 (*preposition*) on top of
2 (*adverb*) more than
3 (*adjective*) finished

CHECK YOUR COMPREHENSION

Read the passage again and answer the questions. Circle your answers.

MAIN IDEA

1. What is the main topic of this passage?
   A. Sign language
   B. School
   C. A special student and her teacher
   D. The zoo

DETAIL

2. How long has Francine Patterson taught Koko?
   A. For one year
   B. For 19 years
   C. For more than 30 years
   D. For 72 years

3. In 1972, what was Francine Patterson?
   A. A school teacher
   B. A university professor
   C. A published author
   D. A psychology student

4. Where did Francine Patterson first meet Koko?
   A. At a zoo
   B. At a university
   C. In Japan
   D. In a classroom

5. What is true about Koko?
   A. She understands Japanese.
   B. She lives in Africa.
   C. She plays with fireworks.
   D. She communicates with sign language.

INFERENCE

6. What do Francine Patterson's friends probably call her?
   A. Dr. Patterson
   B. Penny
   C. Ms. Patterson
   D. Francine

gorillas in the wild

PREPARE TO READ

Discuss these questions.

1. Where do gorillas live?

2. How are people dangerous to gorillas?

WORD FOCUS

Match the words with their definitions.

A.

1. branches __   **a.** a bed for an animal
2. insects __   **b.** a forest in a warm area
3. nest __   **c.** in danger
4. endangered __   **d.** animals with six legs
5. jungle __   **e.** "arms" of trees

B.

1. species __   **a.** kinds of animals
2. cut down __   **b.** away from danger
3. plant __   **c.** cut something to make it fall
4. safe __   **d.** something that grows out of the ground
5. the wild __   **e.** an area far away from cities and people

SCAN

A. Guess if this is true or false. Circle *a* or *b*.

Gorillas live in large groups.

a. True   *b.* False

B. Scan the passage quickly to check your answer.

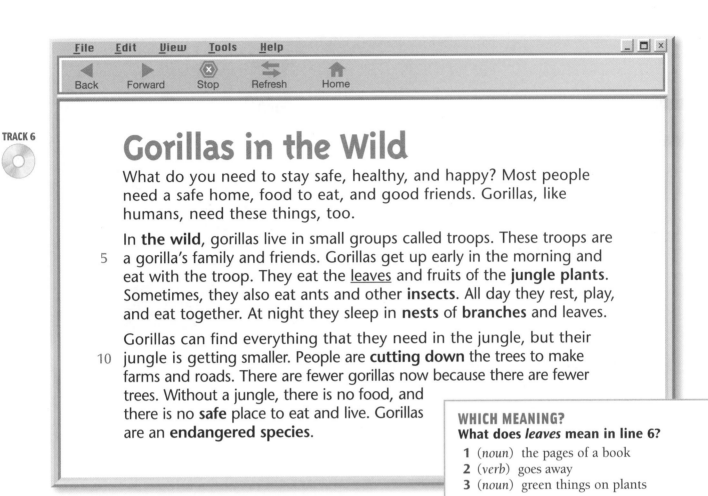

Gorillas in the Wild

What do you need to stay safe, healthy, and happy? Most people need a safe home, food to eat, and good friends. Gorillas, like humans, need these things, too.

In **the wild**, gorillas live in small groups called troops. These troops are
5   a gorilla's family and friends. Gorillas get up early in the morning and eat with the troop. They eat the <u>leaves</u> and fruits of the **jungle plants**. Sometimes, they also eat ants and other **insects**. All day they rest, play, and eat together. At night they sleep in **nests** of **branches** and leaves.

Gorillas can find everything that they need in the jungle, but their
10   jungle is getting smaller. People are **cutting down** the trees to make farms and roads. There are fewer gorillas now because there are fewer trees. Without a jungle, there is no food, and there is no **safe** place to eat and live. Gorillas are an **endangered species**.

WHICH MEANING?
What does *leaves* **mean in line 6?**

1 (*noun*) the pages of a book
2 (*verb*) goes away
3 (*noun*) green things on plants

CHECK YOUR COMPREHENSION

Read the passage again and answer the questions. Circle your answers.

MAIN IDEA

1. What is the main topic of this passage?

A. The way gorillas live in the jungle
B. Plants of the jungle
C. Different endangered species
D. Food for gorillas

DETAIL

2. What is a troop?

A. A house for a gorilla
B. A group of gorillas
C. A special place in the jungle
D. A small gorilla

3. What do gorillas NOT eat?

A. Fruit
B. Insects
C. People
D. Leaves

4. Why do people cut down trees?

A. To eat the fruit
B. To build roads
C. To find the gorillas
D. To make nests

INFERENCE

5. What do gorillas need to live?

A. Trees
B. Farms
C. Roads
D. People

TEXT REFERENCE

6. In line 7, *All day they rest, play, and eat together,* what does the word *they* refer to?

A. Insects
B. Farmers
C. Gorillas
D. Troops

THINGS

Koko uses sign language

PREPARE TO READ
Discuss these questions.

1. What do you think Koko likes to talk about?

2. What questions would you like to ask Koko?

WORD FOCUS
Match the words with their definitions.

A.

1. doll __
2. favorite __
3. ill __
4. pain __
5. toothache __

a. a hurting tooth
b. the thing you like best
c. hurt
d. a toy baby
e. sick

B.

1. set free __
2. sign __
3. terrible __
4. tofu __
5. whale __

a. food made from soy beans
b. a large sea animal
c. let an animal return to the wild
d. use sign language
e. very bad

SCAN
A. Guess the answer. Circle *a* or *b*.

How many signs can Koko use?

a. 100   *b.* 1,000

B. Scan the passage quickly to check your answer.

KOKO

Koko was born in 1971 in a zoo in California. Koko understands 2,000 English words and can use 1,000 signs. She can communicate many things. She can **sign** things like "I am hungry," "I want to eat **tofu**," or "I feel
5   **ill**." Once, Koko had a bad tooth. She was able to let people know that she was in **pain** and needed help. She signed, "I have a **toothache** and the pain is **terrible**."

Koko has many **favorite** things. Her favorite color is red. Her favorite foods are nuts, apples, and corn. She also
10   loves tofu. She likes to draw, write, and play with **dolls**.

Koko likes to watch TV. Her favorite TV shows are about animals in the wild. Her favorite movie is *Free Willy*. It's about a **whale** named Willy. He lived with humans. One
15   day, a little boy **set** him **free**. Maybe Koko wants to go back to the wild, too.

> **WHICH MEANING?**
> **What does *watch* mean in line 11?**
> 1 (*verb*) look at
> 2 (*noun*) small clock
> 3 (*verb*) care for

CHECK YOUR COMPREHENSION

Read the passage again and answer the questions. Circle your answers.

MAIN IDEA

1. What is the main topic of this passage?

   A. Koko's toothache
   B. Koko's food
   C. Koko's activities
   D. Koko's friends

DETAIL

2. How many English words does Koko understand?

   A. 71
   B. 1,000
   C. 1,971
   D. 2,000

3. Koko likes TV shows about

   A. wild animals.
   B. dolls.
   C. animals in the zoo.
   D. food.

4. Who is Willy?

   A. A whale in a movie
   B. Koko's best friend
   C. Koko's helper
   D. A little boy

INFERENCE

5. What does Koko like to do?

   A. Cook
   B. Work
   C. Eat
   D. Read

TEXT REFERENCE

6. In line 12, *It's about a whale named Willy*, what does the word *It* refer to?

   A. An animal
   B. A movie
   C. A TV show
   D. A toy

VOCABULARY REVIEW

CROSSWORD PUZZLE
Complete the crossword using the clues.

Across

3. a toothache is an example of this

5. This type of species is in danger.

7. not in danger

8. a place where baby birds live

Down

1. the "arms" of a tree

2. friends and family members call you by this name

4. very small animals

6. a toy baby

WORDS IN CONTEXT
Fill in the blanks with words from each box.

leaves	zoo	fireworks	insects	nests

1. The _____ is a good place to see different kinds of animals.

2. _____ are small animals with six legs.

3. We can often see _____ in the sky on holidays.

4. In cold places, the _____ fall off the trees before winter.

5. It's interesting to watch birds make their _____ in the spring.

sign language	species	wild	plants	cut down

6. _____ need sun and water to grow.

7. Koko uses _____ because she can't talk with her mouth.

8. House cats don't live in the _____.

9. Birds aren't all the same. There are many different _____.

10. People _____ trees because they want to make roads.

research	dolls	jungle	branches	signed

11. Gorillas like to play in the _____ of trees.
12. Koko _____, "I'm hungry now. I want some tofu."
13. Little children like to play with _____.
14. Dr. Patterson did a lot of _____ on gorillas.
15. Many different kinds of animals live in the _____.

WORD FAMILIES
Fill in the blanks with words from each box.

safety (*noun*)	**safe** (*adjective*)	**safely** (*adverb*)

1. Nests give animals _____.
2. It isn't _____ to play with wild animals.

psychology (*noun*)	**psychologist** (*noun*)	**psychological** (*adjective*)

3. A _____ studies people's thoughts and feelings.
4. Penny studied _____ at a university in California.

communication (*noun*)	**communicate** (*verb*)	**communicative** (*adjective*)

5. Koko loves to talk. She's a very _____ animal.
6. If you learn sign language, you can _____ with Koko.

SYNONYMS OR ANTONYMS?
Look at the word pairs. Are the words synonyms, antonyms, or neither?
Check the correct answer.

		Synonyms	Antonyms	Neither
1. terrible	good	☐	☐	☐
2. pain	hurt	☐	☐	☐
3. ill	sick	☐	☐	☐
4. whale	gorilla	☐	☐	☐
5. safe	dangerous	☐	☐	☐
6. jungle	beach	☐	☐	☐
7. human	person	☐	☐	☐
8. watch	look at	☐	☐	☐
9. tofu	rice	☐	☐	☐
10. set free	keep	☐	☐	☐

SENTENCE COMPLETION
Complete the postcard with words from the box.

endangered	feel	terrible	over	gorillas	favorite

Dear Aunt Myra,

Today we visited the zoo. It was fun to see all the animals there. It's a very big place. It has _____ 300 animals. Do you want to know which my _____ animals were? They were the _____, of course! Did you know that they are an _____ species? That's because people are making roads and towns in their jungles. I _____ sad about that. It's a _____ problem. But, I had a good time today. I hope to see you soon.

Love,

Ricky

WHAT ABOUT YOU?
Speaking
Ask your partner these questions.

1. What is your favorite animal in the zoo?

2. What is your nickname?

3. What do you do when you have a toothache?

4. How do you feel before a test?

5. What TV programs do you like to watch?

Writing
Now write about your partner. Use your partner's answers to the questions.
Example: <u>Ricky's favorite animal is the tiger.</u>

1. _____

2. _____

3. _____

4. _____

5. _____

READING QUIZ

Read the passage and answer the questions. Circle your answers.

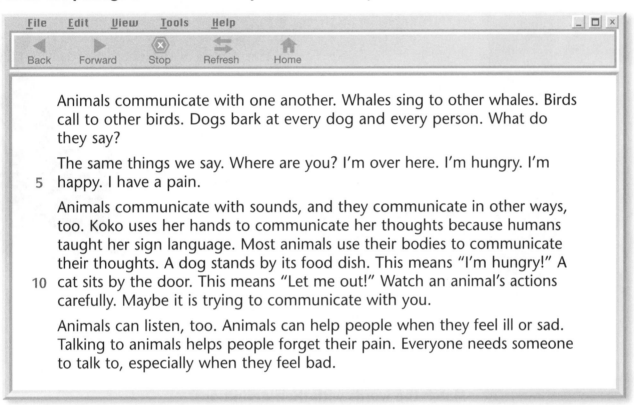

File   Edit   View   Tools   Help

Back   Forward   Stop   Refresh   Home

Animals communicate with one another. Whales sing to other whales. Birds call to other birds. Dogs bark at every dog and every person. What do they say?

The same things we say. Where are you? I'm over here. I'm hungry. I'm
5   happy. I have a pain.

Animals communicate with sounds, and they communicate in other ways, too. Koko uses her hands to communicate her thoughts because humans taught her sign language. Most animals use their bodies to communicate their thoughts. A dog stands by its food dish. This means "I'm hungry!" A
10   cat sits by the door. This means "Let me out!" Watch an animal's actions carefully. Maybe it is trying to communicate with you.

Animals can listen, too. Animals can help people when they feel ill or sad. Talking to animals helps people forget their pain. Everyone needs someone to talk to, especially when they feel bad.

MAIN IDEA

1. What is a good title for this passage?

  A. Helping Sick People

  B. Animal Communication

  C. How to Learn Sign Language

  D. Animals are Smart

DETAIL

2. How does a cat tell you it wants to go outside?

  A. It stands next to its dish.

  B. It uses sign language.

  C. It calls to other cats.

  D. It sits near a door.

INFERENCE

3. Animals communicate

  A. only with other animals.

  B. in many ways.

  C. only when they are hungry.

  D. with words.

VOCABULARY

4. What does *whales* in line 1 mean?

  A. A type of bird

  B. Children

  C. Musicians

  D. A type of sea animal

5. What does *ill* in line 12 mean?

  A. Sick

  B. Hungry

  C. Angry

  D. Tired

TEXT REFERENCE

6. In *This means "I'm hungry!"* in line 9, what does the word *I* refer to?

  A. A dog

  B. A cat

  C. A person

  D. Koko

MOUNTAINS

PEOPLE

PREPARE TO READ

Discuss these questions.

1. Do you like mountain climbing? Why or why not?

2. What are some difficulties of mountain climbing?

WORD FOCUS

Match the words with their definitions.

A.

1. blind __   **a.** go up
2. climb __   **b.** more than usual
3. disabilities __   **c.** can't see
4. especially __   **d.** in spite of; even considering
5. despite __   **e.** problems that make you unable
                         to do some things

B.

1. reach __   **a.** get to (a place)
2. fail __   **b.** a special chair for people who can't walk
3. proud __   **c.** the top of a mountain
4. summit __   **d.** not do something that you want to do
5. wheelchair __   **e.** happy about something that you did

SCAN

A. Guess the answer. Circle *a* or *b*.

Where is Mount Kilimanjaro?

a. Africa   *b.* New Zealand

B. Scan the passage quickly to check your answer.

THREE SPECIAL CLIMBERS

In 2002, three men—two Koreans and a New Zealander—wanted to **climb** Mount Kilimanjaro, the tallest mountain in Africa. Many people try to climb this 5,895-meter-high mountain but **fail**. For these three men, it was **especially** difficult. Kim Hong-bin has no hands. Kim So-young is **blind**.
5 Tony Christianson has no legs. Together the three climbers were each other's eyes, feet, and hands.

It is difficult to climb Mt. Kilimanjaro for a person with eyes, feet, and hands. Imagine climbing this mountain when you can't <u>see</u>, walk, or hold things. Tony Christianson was in a **wheelchair**. Kim Hong-bin pulled him,
10 and Kim So-young pushed him.

All three **reached** 4,700 meters, but they were too tired to continue. After resting, the two Koreans continued on their own and reached the **summit**. They were sad to leave their friend behind, but they were **proud** to reach the summit. They lived
15 their dream **despite** their **disabilities**.

> **WHICH MEANING?**
> **What does *see* mean in line 8?**
> **1** (*verb*) use one's eyes
> **2** (*verb*) visit
> **3** (*verb*) understand

CHECK YOUR COMPREHENSION

Read the passage again and answer the questions. Circle your answers.

MAIN IDEA

1. What is the passage mainly about?
   A. A visit to Africa
   B. People with disabilities
   C. A long climb
   D. Mount Kilimanjaro

DETAIL

2. How tall is Mount Kilimanjaro?
   A. 2,002 meters
   B. 4,700 meters
   C. Almost 6,000 meters
   D. Over 6,000 meters

3. What can't Kim So-young do?
   A. See
   B. Walk
   C. Hold things
   D. Climb mountains

4. What did Tony Christianson do?
   A. He reached the top of the mountain.
   B. He climbed to 4,700 meters.
   C. He waited at the bottom of the mountain.
   D. He climbed to 5,895 meters.

5. How did Kim Hong-bin and Kim So-young feel when they reached the summit?
   A. Angry
   B. Afraid
   C. Proud
   D. Unhappy

INFERENCE

6. Where is Tony Christianson from?
   A. Korea
   B. New Zealand
   C. Africa
   D. Mount Kilimanjaro

PLACES

Mount Kilimanjaro, one of the Seven Summits

PREPARE TO READ
Discuss these questions.

1. What is the tallest mountain in your country? Name some other tall mountains.

2. Why do people like to climb mountains?

WORD FOCUS
Match the words with their definitions.

A.
1. adventure __
2. achievement __
3. continent __
4. pole __
5. peak __

a. the top of a mountain
b. a fun, exciting, but dangerous thing to do
c. the top or bottom of the world
d. finishing something successfully
e. a large piece of land; There are seven in the world.

B.
1. goal __
2. record __
3. Earth __
4. challenge __
5. extra __

a. the world
b. more
c. something you want to do
d. a difficult thing to do
e. write down information

SCAN
A. Guess the answer. Circle *a* or *b*.

The tallest mountain in the world is

a. Mount Everest.   *b.* Mount Kilimanjaro.

B. Scan the passage quickly to check your answer.

The Seven Summits

The **goal** of many mountain climbers is to climb the tallest mountain on each of the seven **continents**. The shortest **peak** is Carstensz Pyramid in Indonesia (4,884 meters), and the tallest is Mount Everest in Nepal (8,850 meters). Since 1986, when climbers started to **record** their **achievements**,
5 over 80 people have climbed all seven summits. The youngest person to climb all seven is Japanese climber Atsushi Yamada. He did it when he was 23 years old.

After climbing the tallest mountains in the world, some climbers also want an **extra challenge**. They want to go to the coldest places on **Earth**, <u>too</u>.
10 This is called the **Adventure** Grand Slam. This means climbing all seven summits and walking to the North and South **Poles**. Korean climber Heo Young-ho climbed all seven summits and went to both poles. In fact, he climbed Mt. Everest twice and went to the poles twice.

WHICH MEANING?
What does _too_ mean in line 9?
1 (_adverb_) also
2 (_adverb_) very
3 (_adverb_) more than enough

TRACK 9

CHECK YOUR COMPREHENSION

Read the passage again and answer the questions. Circle your answers.

MAIN IDEA

1. What is this passage mainly about?
   A. A Japanese climber
   B. Climbing the tallest mountains in the world
   C. The youngest climbers
   D. Traveling to cold places

DETAIL

2. Where is Carstensz Pyramid?
   A. Nepal
   B. The South Pole
   C. Korea
   D. Indonesia

3. How many people have climbed all seven summits?
   A. 23
   B. 80
   C. more than 80
   D. 4,884

4. Which of the following is NOT part of the Adventure Grand Slam?
   A. Climbing seven mountains
   B. Going to Japan
   C. Walking to the North Pole
   D. Going to cold places

INFERENCE

5. What can we guess about Heo Young-ho?
   A. He likes adventure.
   B. He's very young.
   C. He doesn't like the cold.
   D. He isn't strong.

TEXT REFERENCE

6. In line 9, _They want to go to the coldest places on Earth_, what does the word the word _They_ refer to?
   A. Some climbers
   B. The tallest mountains
   C. Korean climbers
   D. The Seven Summits

THINGS

PREPARE TO READ
Discuss these questions.

1. Imagine the top of Mount Everest. What do you think it looks like?

2. What do climbers take up the mountains with them?

WORD FOCUS
Match the words with their definitions.

A.
1. energy __
2. ground __
3. trash __
4. oxygen __
5. pile __

  a. land that you stand on
  b. part of the air
  c. things you don't need anymore
  d. power
  e. a lot of things on top of each other

B.
1. pick up __
2. rip __
3. take away __
4. tent __
5. several __

  a. some
  b. take to another place
  c. take from the ground
  d. tear
  e. a place for climbers to sleep

SCAN
A. Guess the answer. Circle *a* or *b*.

How many people climb Mount Everest every year?

a. 40   *b*. 400

B. Scan the passage quickly to check your answer.

Litter on Mount Everest

Mount Everest is the highest mountain in the world. It is also the highest **trash pile** in the world. About 400 people try to reach the summit every year. This many climbers means a lot of trash.

It is very dangerous to climb Mt. Everest. The air is very thin and cold.
5 Most people carry bottles of **oxygen**; they could die without it. When the oxygen bottles are empty, people throw them on the **ground**. When strong winds **rip** their **tents**, people leave them behind. They don't have the **energy** to **take** their trash **away**. They only have enough energy to go down the mountain safely.

10 Trash is a terrible problem. Since people first began to climb Mt. Everest, they have left 50,000 kilos of trash on the mountain. **Several** groups have climbed the mountain <u>just</u> to **pick up** the trash.
When people plan to climb the mountain, they have to plan to take away their trash.

> **WHICH MEANING?**
> **What does *just* mean in line 12?**
> **1** (*adverb*) exactly
> **2** (*adjective*) fair; honest
> **3** (*adverb*) only

CHECK YOUR COMPREHENSION

Read the passage again and answer the questions. Circle your answers.

MAIN IDEA

1. What is the main topic of the passage?
   A. Wind on the mountain
   B. A problem with trash
   C. A dangerous mountain
   D. Climbing safely

DETAIL

2. Where do climbers put their empty oxygen bottles?
   A. On the ground
   B. In trash cans
   C. On their backs
   D. In their tents

3. Why do climbers leave their trash on the mountain?
   A. Special groups will pick it up.
   B. The wind will blow it away.
   C. They don't have the energy to take it away.
   D. Other climbers will use it later.

4. How much trash is on the mountain?
   A. Four hundred kilos
   B. Four thousand kilos
   C. Five thousand kilos
   D. Fifty thousand kilos

INFERENCE

5. Why do climbers on Mount Everest carry bottles of oxygen?
   A. The weather is cold.
   B. Climbing makes them tired.
   C. The air is very thin.
   D. They are thirsty.

TEXT REFERENCE

6. In line 7, *people leave them behind*, what does the word *them* refer to?
   A. Tents
   B. Oxygen bottles
   C. Strong winds
   D. Other climbers

VOCABULARY REVIEW

MYSTERY PHRASE

Fill in the blanks to complete the sentences. Then use the letters in the circles to fill out the mystery phrase below. Hint: The circles are in the correct order.

1. You have to c l (⃝) b for several days to reach the top of Mt. Kilimanjaro.

2. You sleep in a ☐ e n (⃝) when you are on the mountain.

3. Remember to r (⃝) ☐ o r ☐ your time.

4. Getting to the summit is an a d (⃝) ☐ t ☐ r ☐ .

5. Some people with d ☐ s ☐ b ☐ l ☐ t ☐ (⃝) s use wheelchairs.

6. You need lots of e ☐ e (⃝) g ☐ to climb the Seven Summits.

7. It is a ☐ h a ☐ l (⃝) n g ☐ to reach the peak.

8. D ☐ (⃝) p ☐ t e the trash, the mountain was beautiful.

9. The blind climber was proud of his a c ☐ ☐ e v e ☐ e n (⃝) .

Mystery phrase:

It is a challenge to climb safely to the peak of (⃝)(⃝) . (⃝)(⃝)(⃝)(⃝)(⃝)(⃝)(⃝) .

WORDS IN CONTEXT

Fill in the blanks with words from each box.

disabilities	especially	pick up	record	extra

1. Mt. Everest is the tallest in the world. It's an _____ difficult mountain to climb.

2. Wear an _____ sweater because it's very cold today.

3. Many people have _____. For example, they can't hear, see, or walk.

4. If you want to remember something, you can _____ it.

5. It's a good idea to _____ your things. Don't leave them on the floor.

too	pile	despite	ground	ripped

6. I _____ my shirt, and now it has a big hole.

7. It was the middle of winter, but we slept outside _____ the cold weather.

8. I climbed Kilimanjaro. Now I want to climb Everest, _____.

9. After it rains, the _____ is very wet.

10. We put all our books on top of each other in a _____.

| peak | trash | reached | continents | take away |

11. It's cold and windy on the mountain _____.

12. Please _____ this food. I can't eat any more.

13. Keep the classroom clean. Put your _____ in the can.

14. We drove all day and _____ the city in the evening.

15. I would like to visit all the _____ of the world.

WORD FAMILIES

Fill in the blanks with words from each box.

| adventure (*noun*) | adventurer (*noun*) | adventurous (*adjective*) |

1. _____ people like to climb tall mountains.

2. Climbing mountains is a big _____.

| failure (*noun*) | fail (*verb*) | failing (*adjective*) |

3. You won't be happy if you get a _____ grade on your test.

4. Don't worry if you _____ to reach your goal. You can try again.

| energy (*noun*) | energize (*verb*) | energetic (*adjective*) |

5. You need a lot of _____ to climb a mountain.

6. _____ people like to be busy.

TRUE OR FALSE?

Are the following sentences true or false? Circle your answers.

1. Wheelchairs are for people who can walk.	TRUE	FALSE
2. Blind people can't see.	TRUE	FALSE
3. You will feel proud if you fail your test.	TRUE	FALSE
4. The summit is near the bottom of the mountain.	TRUE	FALSE
5. Mountain climbers sleep in tents.	TRUE	FALSE
6. We need oxygen to live.	TRUE	FALSE
7. The Earth has four poles—North, South, East, and West.	TRUE	FALSE
8. There are just four continents in the world.	TRUE	FALSE

SENTENCE COMPLETION
Complete the notice with words from the box.

pick up	climb	tent	ground	take away	summit

Welcome to Mountain Park

We want our park to stay nice. Please:

1. Don't leave trash on the _____. _____ your trash and put it in a bag.

2. Bring your own _____ if you want to sleep in the park.

3. Make plans if you want to go up the mountain. It takes five hours to reach the _____. Don't _____ alone. Always go with other people.

4. Don't leave anything in the park. _____ your trash and all your things.

Have a good time!

WHAT ABOUT YOU?
Speaking
Ask your partner these questions.

1. When do you feel proud?

2. What is one of your achievements?

3. What goals do you have?

4. What is an especially fun thing that you like to do?

5. When have you slept in a tent?

Writing
Now write about your partner. Use your partner's answers to the questions.
Example: <u>Mary feels proud when she wins a tennis game.</u>

1. _____

2. _____

3. _____

4. _____

5. _____

READING QUIZ

Read the passage and answer the questions. Circle your answers.

People want to climb Mount Everest because it's the highest mountain in the world. Climbing Mount Everest is a difficult challenge. The summit is a very dangerous place. It's always very cold and windy. There isn't much oxygen in the air. No plants or animals can live there. It's also difficult for
5 people to be there. They can't stay on the summit for a long time.

Despite the danger, many people try to climb Mount Everest. Edmund Hillary and Tenzing Norgay were the first people to reach the summit. Edmund Hillary was from New Zealand. Tenzing Norgay grew up near Mount Everest. He tried to reach the top several times, but he failed.
10 Finally, on May 29, 1953, he climbed to the summit with Edmund Hillary. This achievement made Hillary and Norgay famous all around the world. Since then, many other climbers have reached the summit, but many others have failed.

MAIN IDEA

1. What is the main topic of this passage?

   A. Edmund Hillary and Tenzing Norgay
   B. Climbing Mount Everest
   C. Weather on Mount Everest
   D. Mountain plants and animals

DETAIL

2. What can you see at the top of Mount Everest?

   A. Plants
   B. Animals
   C. Houses
   D. None of the above

3. What is true about Tenzing Norgay?

   A. He's from New Zealand.
   B. He tried to climb Mount Everest several times.
   C. He never reached the top of Mount Everest.
   D. He doesn't like climbing.

INFERENCE

4. Why do people climb Mount Everest?

   A. They want to spend several days at the summit.
   B. They want a difficult challenge.
   C. They want to see the plants and animals.
   D. They want to meet Edmund Hillary.

VOCABULARY

5. What does *oxygen* in line 4 mean?

   A. Wind
   B. Light from the sun
   C. Part of the air
   D. Cold

6. What does *several* in line 9 mean?

   A. One
   B. Two
   C. A few
   D. Very many

MYSTERY

PEOPLE

PREPARE TO READ
Discuss these questions.

1. Do you know the man in the picture? What do you know about him?

2. Do you like mystery stories? Which ones do you know?

WORD FOCUS
Match the words with their definitions.

A.
1. clue __
2. create __
3. crime __
4. escape __
5. fans __

a. get away
b. a small piece of information
c. people who like a famous person
d. make (something new)
e. a bad thing to do

B.
1. detective __
2. mystery __
3. popular __
4. single __
5. solve __

a. one
b. find the answer
c. something we don't know or understand
d. a person who looks for the answer to crimes
e. many people like it

SCAN
A. Guess the answer. Circle *a* or *b*.

Where does Sherlock Holmes live?

a. New York   *b.* London

B. Scan the passage quickly to check your answer.

A Famous Detective

Who is this man? He can **solve** a **crime** with a **single clue**. He smokes a pipe, and he can <u>play</u> the violin. He lives on Baker Street in London. His best friend is Dr. Watson.

He's Sherlock Holmes, the famous **detective created** by Sir
5 Arthur Conan Doyle.

Between 1887 and 1927, Sir Arthur wrote four novels and 56 short stories about Sherlock Holmes and Dr. Watson. After so many stories, he became tired of Holmes. He wrote one story in which someone killed Holmes. Sherlock Holmes' **fans** were
10 very unhappy about this. Sir Arthur had to write a new story about Holmes' **escape** from death.

The Sherlock Holmes stories are still **popular** today. Some fans seem to think that Sherlock Holmes is real. People send letters to his address on Baker Street. They
15 ask him to solve real crimes. Maybe the real **mystery** is: Why do people write letters to a storybook character?

WHICH MEANING?
What does *play* mean in line 2?
1 (*verb*) make music
2 (*noun*) something in a theater
3 (*verb*) be part of a game

CHECK YOUR COMPREHENSION

Read the passage again and answer the questions. Circle your answers.

MAIN IDEA

1. What is this passage mainly about?

A. Sir Arthur Conan Doyle
B. A famous storybook character
C. A house on Baker Street
D. Letters to Sherlock Holmes

DETAIL

2. Who is Dr. Watson?

A. A writer
B. A violin player
C. A friend of Sherlock Holmes
D. A famous detective

3. What is NOT true about Sherlock Holmes?

A. He lives on Baker Street.
B. He smokes a pipe.
C. He writes stories.
D. He solves crimes.

4. When did Sir Arthur Conan Doyle begin writing about Sherlock Holmes?

A. 1856
B. 1887
C. 1927
D. 1956

5. How many novels did Sir Arthur write about Sherlock Holmes?

A. 4
B. 27
C. 56
D. 60

INFERENCE

6. Why did Sir Arthur become tired of writing about Sherlock Holmes?

A. Nobody bought his books.
B. The stories were very long.
C. He didn't have time to read all the letters from fans.
D. He wrote a lot of stories.

PLACES

Stonehenge

PREPARE TO READ
Discuss these questions.

1. Where is this place?

2. What is this place used for?

WORD FOCUS
Match the words with their definitions.

A.
1. ancient __   **a.** something that shows the months of the year
2. builder __   **b.** very, very old
3. calendar __   **c.** many kilos
4. heavy __   **d.** the power of the Earth, not of people
5. nature __   **e.** a person who builds things

B.
1. purpose __   **a.** rock
2. religious __   **b.** about faith, belief, or worship
3. season __   **c.** a dark area
4. shadow __   **d.** reason
5. stone __   **e.** a part of the year

SCAN
A. Guess the answer. Circle *a* or *b*.

How old is Stonehenge?

a. 400 years   *b.* 4,500 years

B. Scan the passage quickly to check your answer.

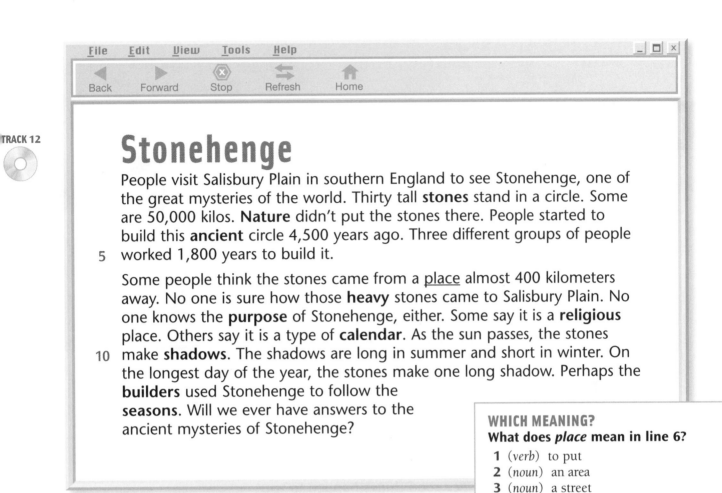

Stonehenge

People visit Salisbury Plain in southern England to see Stonehenge, one of the great mysteries of the world. Thirty tall **stones** stand in a circle. Some are 50,000 kilos. **Nature** didn't put the stones there. People started to build this **ancient** circle 4,500 years ago. Three different groups of people
5 worked 1,800 years to build it.

Some people think the stones came from a <u>place</u> almost 400 kilometers away. No one is sure how those **heavy** stones came to Salisbury Plain. No one knows the **purpose** of Stonehenge, either. Some say it is a **religious** place. Others say it is a type of **calendar**. As the sun passes, the stones
10 make **shadows**. The shadows are long in summer and short in winter. On the longest day of the year, the stones make one long shadow. Perhaps the **builders** used Stonehenge to follow the **seasons**. Will we ever have answers to the ancient mysteries of Stonehenge?

WHICH MEANING?
What does *place* mean in line 6?
1 (*verb*) to put
2 (*noun*) an area
3 (*noun*) a street

CHECK YOUR COMPREHENSION

Read the passage again and answer the questions. Circle your answers.

MAIN IDEA

1. What is the main topic of this passage?

  A. Heavy stones

  B. Seasons of the year

  C. A mysterious place in England

  D. Long and short shadows

DETAIL

2. What is Stonehenge?

  A. A religious place

  B. A calendar

  C. Both a religious place and a calendar

  D. No one knows.

3. How many years ago was Stonehenge completed?

  A. 1,800

  B. 2,700

  C. 4,500

  D. 50,000

4. How many stones are there at Stonehenge?

  A. 30

  B. 50

  C. 400

  D. 4,000

INFERENCE

5. What is true about Stonehenge?

  A. Many people visit it.

  B. It's a new place.

  C. One group built it.

  D. It's closed in the summer.

TEXT REFERENCE

6. In line 2, *Some are 50,000*, what does the word *Some* refer to?

  A. Shadows

  B. Tall stones

  C. Old cities

  D. Ancient circles

THINGS

PREPARE TO READ

Discuss these questions.

1. Every year some children are missing. How do police look for them?

2. Can mind readers or people with other special powers of the mind help the police?

WORD FOCUS

Match the words with their definitions.

A.
1. arrest __
2. correct __
3. everywhere __
4. guess __
5. lucky __

   a. in every place
   b. right; not wrong
   c. good things happen to you
   d. take to the police station
   e. try to find the right answer

B.
1. missing __
2. psychic __
3. relative __
4. search __
5. woods __

   a. look for
   b. lost
   c. an area with a lot of trees
   d. a person who can read minds
   e. a person in your family

SCAN

A. Guess if this is true or false. Circle *a* or *b*.

Police sometimes ask psychics for help.

a. True   *b.* False

B. Scan the passage quickly to check your answer.

MISSING

A boy is **missing**. He hasn't come home for several days. The police **search everywhere**, but they find nothing. Finally, the family asks a **psychic** detective for help.

5 The psychic holds the missing boy's shoe. She says she feels the boy's energy. She sees pictures in her <u>mind</u>. She sees a tent in the **woods** and a woman with a dog. Later, the police find the missing boy in the woods. They **arrest** a woman with a dog. Did the psychic solve the crime?

Many people say that the answer is "yes." Often, **relatives** of missing people ask psychics for help. Even police sometimes use the help of psychics.

10 Many others say that psychics can't really solve crimes. They say that psychics just make **lucky guesses**. But if this guess is **correct**, a missing person could be found. The police and the family of missing people need all the help they can get.

WHICH MEANING?
What does *mind* mean in line 5?

1 (*verb*) to pay attention to
2 (*noun*) thoughts
3 (*verb*) be careful about

CHECK YOUR COMPREHENSION

Read the passage again and answer the questions. Circle your answers.

MAIN IDEA

1. What is the main topic of this passage?

A. A lost boy
B. Psychic detectives
C. Solving crimes
D. A tent in the woods

DETAIL

2. What does the psychic do with the lost boy's shoe?

A. She wears it for a week.
B. She sells it.
C. She holds it in her hand.
D. She cleans it.

3. Where did the police find the lost boy?

A. In his bedroom
B. At a psychic's house
C. In the woods
D. At the police station

4. Who asks psychics for help?

A. Missing people
B. Women with dogs
C. Lost people's families
D. Relatives of police

INFERENCE

5. How does a psychic find a missing person?

A. She wears special shoes.
B. She sleeps in a tent.
C. She uses her mind.
D. She calls the police.

TEXT REFERENCE

6. In line 4, *She says she feels the boy's energy*, what does the word *She* refer to?

A. The boy's relative
B. The psychic
C. A woman with a dog
D. A police officer

VOCABULARY REVIEW

WORD SEARCH
Find and circle the vocabulary below.

clue
detective
lucky
mystery
psychic
season
shadow
single
solve
woods

E	X	F	Y	Y	O	L	X	N	H	A	C	B	S	O
S	V	G	R	A	B	M	O	N	L	I	S	V	H	Z
N	T	I	E	J	P	F	D	X	H	D	E	E	A	S
Y	F	H	T	S	A	Y	K	C	U	L	W	X	D	J
S	J	G	S	C	C	I	Y	C	M	O	Y	O	O	H
S	N	Y	Y	D	E	S	S	Z	I	D	Z	L	W	E
K	D	A	M	G	P	T	M	E	E	F	L	S	A	U
I	K	O	F	R	Y	X	E	V	A	V	W	S	C	L
J	X	R	O	X	N	D	L	D	R	S	O	L	Y	C
S	F	C	K	W	X	W	R	I	S	L	O	E	Z	Z
X	H	S	S	I	G	E	K	G	V	Z	A	N	G	S
R	S	Z	M	U	K	B	Y	E	R	F	I	J	B	M
U	M	F	L	T	H	Y	E	D	X	I	Q	Y	Y	B
F	G	B	T	F	F	Q	V	U	J	V	I	C	G	X
E	T	F	S	I	N	G	L	E	P	O	I	M	B	U

WORDS IN CONTEXT
Fill in the blanks with words from each box.

fans	religious	stone	escaped	ancient

1. A tiger _____ from the zoo yesterday, and it is still missing.

2. A lot of people like Sherlock Holmes. He has a lot of _____.

3. Churches and temples are _____ places.

4. This place is _____. It's thousands of years old.

5. Some people make houses of wood; others make houses of _____.

heavy	psychic	builders	purpose	nature

6. I can't pick up these bags because they are _____.

7. The _____ made this house in just two weeks.

8. Do you believe that a _____ can read your mind?

9. Mountains are made by _____, not by people.

10. The _____ of an umbrella is to keep you dry.

popular	everywhere	searched	arrested	solve

11. Many people visit Stonehenge. It's a _____ place.

12. It was a difficult math problem, but I was able to _____ it.

13. The police _____ that man because he took money from the bank.

14. We _____ all over the house, but we couldn't find the keys.

15. Everybody has a cell phone these days. You see them _____.

WORD FAMILIES
Fill in the blanks with words from each box.

creation (*noun*)	**create** (*verb*)	**creative** (*adjective*)

1. Julie painted a beautiful picture. She is very proud of her _____.

2. She is so _____. She always makes beautiful things.

corrections (*noun*)	**correct** (*verb*)	**correctly** (*adverb*)

3. If you make mistakes, you will have to _____ them.

4. The teacher can help you make _____.

luck (*noun*)	**lucky** (*adjective*)	**luckily** (*adverb*)

5. I need a lot of _____ because I want to win this game.

6. _____ people usually get what they want.

WRONG WORD
One word in each group does not fit. Circle the word.

1. season	cold	calendar	year
2. teachers	cousins	relatives	parents
3. arrest	crime	detective	friend
4. jungle	trees	house	woods
5. one	several	single	alone
6. work	play	music	piano

SENTENCE COMPLETION

Complete the e-mail with words from the box.

correct	missing	guess	everywhere	search

To: Sam
From: Lee
Subject: lost book

Hi Sam,

My math book is _____. I can't find it. I have looked _____ —in my house, at school, and at the park. Maybe it's at your house. Can you please _____ for it there? I need it to study for our test tomorrow. I want all my test answers to be _____. I don't want to _____ the answers, I want to know them. Please help me find my book!

Lee

WHAT ABOUT YOU?
Speaking

Ask your partner these questions.

1. What is your favorite season? Why?

2. What is your favorite place to go on weekends?

3. Which popular singers do you like?

4. Who is your favorite relative?

5. Has something lucky happened to you? What was it?

Writing

Now write about your partner. Use your partner's answers to the questions.

Example: _Bob likes winter because he can play in the snow._

1. _____

2. _____

3. _____

4. _____

5. _____

READING QUIZ

Read the passage and answer the questions. Circle your answers.

Most psychics believe that there is no mystery to psychic ability. Everybody has it. You just have to learn to use it.

There are several ways to begin learning. When the telephone rings, don't answer it quickly. First, try to guess who is calling.
5 When someone knocks on your door, don't open it. Try to guess who is there. Then open the door to see if your guess is correct. You can also use a pile of playing cards. Take one card from the pile. Before you look at it, guess if it's red or black. Continue with all the cards in the pile.

10 You can also try to read a person's mind. Choose a close friend or relative. Ask that person to communicate some thoughts to you. Try to read the thoughts. Don't worry if it seems difficult at the beginning. It takes time to learn.

MAIN IDEA

1. What is a good title for this passage?

A. How to Answer the Telephone

B. Games with Cards

C. Psychic Mysteries

D. Learn to Use Your Psychic Ability

DETAIL

2. How can you use playing cards to learn to use psychic ability?

A. Try to guess the color of the card.

B. Learn how to play a game.

C. Give them to a psychic.

D. Guess who put the cards there.

3. Which is NOT suggested as a way to learn to use psychic ability?

A. Read a book about psychics.

B. Guess who is calling on the telephone.

C. Ask a friend for help.

D. Guess who is knocking on the door.

TEXT REFERENCE

4. In line 2, *You just have to learn to use it*, what does the word *it* refer to?

A. A playing card

B. The telephone

C. Psychic ability

D. A psychic

VOCABULARY

5. What does *correct* in line 7 mean?

A. Right

B. Wrong

C. Easy

D. Difficult

6. What does *relative* in line 11 mean?

A. Classmate

B. Neighbor

C. Coworker

D. Family member

CLOTHES

PEOPLE

fashion model Kate Moss

PREPARE TO READ
Discuss these questions.

1. Would you like to be a fashion model? Why or why not?

2. What is the life of a model like?

WORD FOCUS
Match the words with their definitions.

A.
1. accident __
2. agent __
3. fashion __
4. change (out of) __
5. model __

  a. a person who works showing new clothes
  b. something that is not planned
  c. put on different clothes
  d. a person who finds jobs for others
  e. popular clothes

B.
1. spot __
2. suddenly __
3. thrilled __
4. uniform __
5. wealthiest __

  a. special clothes for school or work
  b. quickly and by surprise
  c. with the most money
  d. see
  e. very excited

SCAN
A. Guess the answer. Circle *a* or *b*.

How old was Kate Moss when she became a model?

a. 14 years old   *b.* 18 years old

B. Scan the passage quickly to check your answer.

Kate Moss

Kate Moss never planned to become a **fashion model**. It happened by **accident**. One day she was on an airplane with her family when an **agent spotted** her. The agent told Moss, "I can get you <u>work</u> as a model." Moss was only 14.

5 Moss visited the agent in London. They took photographs. In just one week, Moss got her first job. She told her friends in school about it. They were **thrilled** to see her picture in a magazine.

She continued to go to school and to model. When she had a job as a model, she took the train to London after school. On 10 the train, she **changed** out of her school **uniform** and put on ordinary clothes. Then, she got a job with Calvin Klein, and her life **changed**. **Suddenly**, her pictures were everywhere. Now, Kate Moss is famous, and she is the **wealthiest** model in Britain.

WHICH MEANING?
What does *work* mean in line 4?
1 (*verb*) run a machine
2 (*noun*) a piece of art
3 (*noun*) a job

CHECK YOUR COMPREHENSION

Read the passage again and answer the questions. Circle your answers.

MAIN IDEA

1. What is the main topic of this passage?

   A. The work of an agent
   B. A famous fashion model
   C. Different kinds of clothes
   D. A fashion magazine

DETAIL

2. Where did the agent first see Kate?

   A. On an airplane
   B. In London
   C. On a train
   D. At school

3. How did Kate travel to London?

   A. By airplane
   B. By train
   C. By car
   D. On foot

4. What did Kate do on the way to London?

   A. She bought new clothes.
   B. She washed her clothes.
   C. She gave away her clothes.
   D. She put on different clothes.

INFERENCE

5. When did Kate first become famous?

   A. When she met the agent on the airplane
   B. When she got her first modeling job
   C. When she got a job with Calvin Klein
   D. When she became the wealthiest model in Britain

TEXT REFERENCE

6. In line 7, *They were thrilled to see her picture in a magazine*, what does the word *They* refer to?

   A. Kate's teachers
   B. Kate's agent
   C. Kate's family
   D. Kate's friends

PLACES

PREPARE TO READ
Discuss these questions.

1. Is it better to have a lot of clothes or a few clothes?

2. Is your closet neat?

WORD FOCUS
Match the words with their definitions.

A.
1. active __
2. artistic __
3. casual __
4. express __
5. hang up __

a. hang in a closet or on a wall
b. always busy
c. communicate feelings or thoughts
d. a word for a person who likes art
e. relaxed; not formal

B.
1. mess __
2. organize __
3. personality __
4. practical __
5. take care of __

a. the kind of person that you are
b. not neat; things out of order
c. useful
d. be careful with; keep nice
e. put things in order

SCAN
A. Guess the answer. Circle *a* or *b*.

Who wrote the first letter?

a. Fashion Lady   *b.* Miss Mess

B. Scan the passage quickly to check your answer.

Ask the Fashion Lady

Dear Fashion Lady,

I love clothes. I have lots of them. My closet is a big **mess**. I can never find my favorite clothes. Please help!

Miss Mess

5 Dear Miss Mess,

You love your clothes, so **take care of** them. First, **hang** them **up**. Then, **organize** them.

There are many ways to organize your clothes. Your clothes **express** your **personality**. If you are **artistic**, you can organize your clothes by 10 color. Then, it will be easy to find your green sweater or black jeans. If you are an **active** person, organize your clothes by activity. Organize them into school clothes, party clothes, sports clothes, and **casual** clothes. Maybe you are a **practical** person. Organize your closet into spring, summer, <u>fall</u>, and winter clothes.

15 Match your organization system to your personality. Then your clothes will match your style and look good on you.

20 Fashion Lady

WHICH MEANING?
What does *fall* mean in line 14?
1 (*verb*) go down
2 (*noun*) a season of the year
3 (*noun*) a place where water goes over rocks

CHECK YOUR COMPREHENSION

Read the passage again and answer the questions. Circle your answers.

MAIN IDEA

1. Why did Miss Mess write the letter?

  A. She wants more clothes.
  B. She takes art classes.
  C. She needs help with her closet.
  D. She's going to a party.

DETAIL

2. What does the Fashion Lady tell Miss Mess to do?

  A. Hang up her clothes
  B. Buy new school clothes
  C. Wear more colors
  D. Wash her clothes

3. What is true about Miss Mess's closet?

  A. It's empty.
  B. It's full of art.
  C. It doesn't have nice clothes.
  D. It isn't organized.

4. How can a practical person organize her clothes?

  A. By color
  B. By activity
  C. By season
  D. By size

INFERENCE

5. Fashion Lady is probably

  A. a relative of Miss Mess.
  B. a writer for a magazine.
  C. a teacher of Miss Mess.
  D. an artist.

TEXT REFERENCE

6. In line 7, *Then, organize them*, what does the word *them* refer to?

  A. Clothes
  B. Jeans
  C. Closets
  D. Ways

THINGS

PREPARE TO READ
Discuss these questions.

1. What kinds of clothes do you wear for school?

2. Do you think school uniforms are a good idea or a bad idea?

WORD FOCUS
Match the words with their definitions.

A.

1. appearance __   **a.** not agree; have a different idea

2. common __   **b.** the same

3. disagree __   **c.** things you have to do; laws

4. equal __   **d.** the way something or someone looks

5. rules __   **e.** usual

B.

1. obey __   **a.** something people have done for many years

2. tradition __   **b.** become

3. turn into __   **c.** do what someone says you have to do

4. unattractive __   **d.** not comfortable

5. uncomfortable __   **e.** not pretty

SCAN
A. Guess if this is true or false. Circle *a* or *b*.

School children in Britain wear uniforms.

a. True   *b.* False

B. Scan the passage quickly to check your answer.

School Uniforms

In many countries, like Britain and Japan, <u>wear</u>ing school uniforms is still a **tradition**, but in others, like the United States, France, and Germany, uniforms are not so **common**.

5 Some people say that uniforms are important. Uniforms help students learn to **obey rules** and learn to study better. They make all the students **equal** in **appearance**. They also help students feel like part of the school.

Other people **disagree**. They say that uniforms are **uncomfortable** and **unattractive**. Most importantly, they say that when students wear uniforms, they can't express themselves with their clothes.

10 Some students think uniforms can be attractive. Some school students make small changes to their uniforms because they want to look more fashionable. They use their uniforms as a way to express themselves. Some students try to attend the school with the best uniform. This is a different way to look at uniforms. An old
15 tradition is **turning into** a new fashion.

WHICH MEANING?
What does *wear* mean in line 1?
1 (*verb*) put on clothes
2 (*noun*) clothes
3 (*verb*) to become old from use

CHECK YOUR COMPREHENSION

Read the passage again and answer the questions. Circle your answers.

MAIN IDEA

1. What is the main topic of this passage?
 A. Schools in different countries
 B. Different kinds of uniforms
 C. Clothes for school
 D. The best schools

DETAIL

2. In which country are uniforms not very common?
 A. Germany
 B. France
 C. The United States
 D. All of the above

3. Why do some people say uniforms are important?
 A. They don't let students express themselves.
 B. They help students study better.
 C. They aren't common.
 D. They look nicer than ordinary clothes.

4. Why don't some people like uniforms?
 A. They're too expensive.
 B. They're different at every school.
 C. They aren't used in all countries.
 D. They aren't attractive.

5. Why do some students make changes to their uniforms?
 A. They want to be fashionable.
 B. Their uniforms aren't comfortable.
 C. They want to attend a different school.
 D. Their uniforms are too small.

INFERENCE

6. People who like uniforms believe it's important to
 A. look attractive.
 B. be fashionable.
 C. attend the best school.
 D. follow rules.

VOCABULARY REVIEW

CROSSWORD PUZZLE
Complete the crossword using the clues.

Across

2. style of clothes for play, not work or school

7. Students must _____ the rules.

8. something that is not planned

Down

1. Wearing school uniforms is a _____ in Britain.

3. a person who finds jobs for a model

4. Kate Moss is one.

5. to put on different clothes

6. how you feel when your clothes are too small

WORDS IN CONTEXT
Fill in the blanks with words from each box.

uniforms	thrilled	mess	hang up	appearance

1. Please _____ your coat in that closet.

2. At our school we can choose our own clothes because we don't have _____.

3. I was _____ when I met a famous model.

4. I like the _____ of students in uniforms. I think they look nice.

5. This room is a _____. We have to organize it.

personality	artistic	casual	model	spotted

6. Everybody likes my teacher because she has such a kind _____.

7. When I _____ this sweater in the store, I knew I wanted to buy it.

8. My party will be _____. You don't have to wear special clothes.

9. Some _____ people like to draw and paint.

10. I want to be a _____ because I love clothes.

uncomfortable	fashion	equal	accident	take care of

11. I'm sorry I broke your plate. It was an _____.

12. These two shirts cost the same. Their prices are _____.

13. I love clothes, so I like to read _____ magazines.

14. If you have nice clothes, _____ them. Hang them up in your closet.

15. My new shoes are very _____ because they're too small for me.

WORD FAMILIES
Fill in the blanks with words from each box.

expression (*noun*)	express (*verb*)	expressive (*adjective*)

1. I know that she is sad because of the _____ on her face.

2. Some people are very _____. It's easy to see their feelings.

organization (*noun*)	organize (*verb*)	organized (*adjective*)

3. My closet isn't _____. I can't find anything.

4. I plan to _____ my clothes by color.

disagreement (*noun*)	disagree (*verb*)	disagreeable (*adjective*)

5. Nobody likes _____ people.

6. My friend and I had a _____, and now we're angry with each other.

SYNONYMS OR ANTONYMS?
Look at the word pairs. Are the words synonyms, antonyms, or neither?
Check the correct answer.

		Synonyms	Antonyms	Neither
1.	unattractive	beautiful	☐	☐	☐
2.	equal	same	☐	☐	☐
3.	agent	model	☐	☐	☐
4.	active	artistic	☐	☐	☐
5.	wealthiest	richest	☐	☐	☐
6.	common	rare	☐	☐	☐
7.	fashion	magazine	☐	☐	☐
8.	work	job	☐	☐	☐
9.	thrilled	bored	☐	☐	☐
10.	spot	see	☐	☐	☐
11.	active	lazy	☐	☐	☐
12.	fall	winter	☐	☐	☐
13.	turn into	become	☐	☐	☐
14.	practical	new	☐	☐	☐
15.	suddenly	slowly	☐	☐	☐

WHAT ABOUT YOU?
Speaking
Ask your partner these questions.
1. What kind of clothes do you like to wear?
2. What kind of clothes are unattractive to you?
3. What are some rules in your classroom?
4. Who is artistic in your family?
5. Who takes care of you when you are sick?

Writing
Now write about your partner. Use your partner's answers to the questions.
Example: <u>Susan likes to wear short skirts and tall boots</u>.

1. _____

2. _____

3. _____

4. _____

5. _____

READING QUIZ

Read the passage and answer the questions. Circle your answers.

Dear School Director,

Next year, the students at our school won't have to wear uniforms. I disagree with this plan. I like wearing my uniform. It helps me feel like part of the school, and it helps me study better. Also, it's very practical
5 because it's easy to take care of.

Some students don't like our school uniforms because they aren't fashionable. I disagree with these students. I don't think a fashionable appearance is important. Some students say our uniforms are uncomfortable. I agree. I think we can make our uniforms more
10 comfortable, but I don't think we should stop wearing them.

Uniforms are a tradition. They are common everywhere. We should continue wearing uniforms at our school.

Sincerely,

Janet Johnson

MAIN IDEA

1. Why did Janet Johnson write this letter?

A. To ask for a new uniform
B. To describe her uniform
C. To express her ideas about uniforms
D. To explain the history of uniforms

DETAIL

2. Why does Janet Johnson like her uniform?

A. It's very comfortable.
B. It helps her study better.
C. It's fashionable.
D. It helps her find friends.

INFERENCE

3. What does Janet Johnson think about school uniforms?

A. They aren't common.
B. They are important for students.
C. They aren't a good idea.
D. They aren't easy to clean.

TEXT REFERENCE

4. In line 6, *they aren't fashionable*, what does the word *they* refer to?

A. Students
B. Uniforms
C. Schools
D. Traditions

VOCABULARY

5. What does *disagree* in line 7 mean?

A. Not like
B. Not care
C. Have a similar idea
D. Have a different idea

6. What does *common* in line 11 mean?

A. Unusual
B. Pretty
C. Usual
D. Useful

SKYSCRAPERS

PEOPLE

Alain Robert climbs a skyscraper

PREPARE TO READ
Discuss these questions.

1. What is this man doing? Do you want to try it?

2. Is climbing buildings illegal? Should it be?

WORD FOCUS
Match the words with their definitions.

A.
1. building __   a. worried
2. concerned __   b. OK to do something
3. hobby __   c. a place to live or work
4. jail __   d. a free time activity
5. permission __   e. a place to lock up people

B.
1. salesman __   a. a tall building
2. stories __   b. opposite of put on; remove shoes or clothes
3. tower __   c. a person who sells things
4. take off __   d. not common
5. unusual __   e. floors of a building

SCAN
A. Guess the answer. Circle *a* or *b*.

How many stories does the Jinmao Tower have?

a. 88   *b.* 108

B. Scan the passage quickly to check your answer.

Alain Robert and Han Qizhi

Alain Robert has a nickname–Spiderman. It comes from his **unusual hobby**. He climbs tall **buildings**. He has climbed more than 30 tall buildings around the world. In 2001, he planned to climb the Jinmao **Tower** in China. It is 88 **stories** tall.

5 Robert made plans. He <u>got</u> special shoes and gloves. However, he couldn't get **permission** to climb. Also, the weather was bad. Robert decided not to climb. It was too dangerous.

A few days later, Han Qizhi walked by the Jinmao Tower. He wasn't a famous climber. He was a shoe **salesman**. He didn't have any plans or special shoes

10 or gloves. He didn't have permission, and he wasn't **concerned** about the weather. He just looked at the tower, **took off** his jacket, and started to climb.

Han felt lucky because he escaped death, but he didn't escape the police. They put him in **jail** for a few days. After that, he decided not to try climbing any more buildings.

WHICH MEANING?
What does *got* mean in line 5?

1 (*verb*) arrived
2 (*verb*) became
3 (*verb*) bought

CHECK YOUR COMPREHENSION

Read the passage again and answer the questions. Circle your answers.

MAIN IDEA

. What is the main topic of this passage?

A. A famous climber
B. The weather in China
C. Climbing a tall building
D. The Jinmao Tower

DETAIL

. How many tall buildings has Alain Robert climbed?

A. More than 30
B. More than 80
C. 88
D. 200

. Why didn't Alain Robert climb the Jinmao Tower?

A. He was too tired.
B. Han Qizhi wanted to climb it first.
C. He couldn't get permission, and the weather was bad.
D. He didn't have special shoes and gloves.

4. What is Han Qizhi's job?

A. Weather man
B. Police officer
C. Building cleaner
D. Salesman

5. Why did Han Qizhi feel lucky?

A. He didn't die.
B. He reached the top of the building.
C. He sold a lot of shoes.
D. He met Alain Robert.

INFERENCE

6. Why did the police put Han Qizhi in jail?

A. He climbed the building without permission.
B. He stole something from Alain Robert.
C. He didn't wear special gloves.
D. He climbed in bad weather.

PLACES

The Taipei 101 Tower

PREPARE TO READ

Discuss these questions.

1. Is this a beautiful building? What makes a building beautiful?

2. What places and things can you find inside a building like this?

WORD FOCUS

Match the words with their definitions.

A.

1. bamboo __	**a.**	shape
2. design __	**b.**	looking at things
3. elevators __	**c.**	a place to exercise
4. observation __	**d.**	a type of plant
5. health club __	**e.**	machines that carry people up and down in buildings

B.

1. section __	**a.**	a tall building
2. skyscraper __	**b.**	below the ground
3. shopping mall __	**c.**	a part or piece
4. underground __	**d.**	things you see
5. views __	**e.**	a group of stores inside a building

SCAN

A. Guess if this is true or false. Circle *a* or *b*.

There are two hotels in the Taipei 101 Tower.

a. True   *b.* False

B. Scan the passage quickly to check your answer.

File   Edit   View   Tools   Help

◀ Back   ▶ Forward   ⊗ Stop   ⇄ Refresh   🏠 Home

The Taipei 101 Tower

The Taipei 101 Tower in Taiwan is one of the tallest buildings in the world. It is 508 meters tall. It has an unusual **design**. It looks like a **bamboo** plant. The lucky number eight is also part of the design. Each **section** of the building has eight <u>floor</u>s.

5   The tower is like a small city. There is parking for more than 1,800 cars **underground**. A **shopping mall** fills several floors. There are two hotels, a **health club**, many restaurants, and a lot of offices.

Near the top of the building—on floors 89 to 91—there are **observation** areas with good **views** of Taipei. You can get to these on some of the

10   world's fastest **elevators**. The elevators travel 1,000 meters a minute. It takes just 39 seconds to get to the 89th floor. From there, you can look down on all the other **skyscrapers** below.

WHICH MEANING?
What does *floor* mean in line 4?

1 (*noun*) a story in a building
2 (*verb*) give a big surprise
3 (*noun*) ground

CHECK YOUR COMPREHENSION

Read the passage again and answer the questions. Circle your answers.

MAIN IDEA

1. What is the main topic of this passage?
   A. A tall building
   B. Fast elevators
   C. Good views
   D. A large shopping mall

DETAIL

2. How tall is the Taipei 101 Tower?
   A. 508 meters
   B. 891 meters
   C. 1,000 meters
   D. 1,800 meters

3. What does the building look like?
   A. A number eight
   B. A large car
   C. A bamboo plant
   D. A small tower

4. What is inside the building?
   A. Parks
   B. Apartments
   C. Offices
   D. All of the above

INFERENCE

5. Why do people go to the top of the Taipei 101 Tower?
   A. To go shopping
   B. To get good luck
   C. To look at bamboo plants
   D. To see views of the city

TEXT REFERENCE

6. In line 12, *From there, you can look down on all the other skyscrapers below*, what does the word *there* refer to?
   A. The elevators
   B. The 89th floor of the tower
   C. Other skyscrapers
   D. Restaurants

THINGS

PREPARE TO READ
Discuss these questions.

1. What materials do people use to build skyscrapers?

2. What is the tallest building you have visited?

WORD FOCUS
Match the words with their definitions.

A.
1. brick ___
2. construct ___
3. iron ___
4. materials ___
5. support ___

a. things you use to make something
b. hold something up
c. a block, like a stone, used for building
d. build
e. a strong, heavy metal

B.
1. technology ___
2. steel ___
3. wall ___
4. passenger ___
5. invention ___

a. the side of a building
b. a strong, light metal
c. a person who travels by plane, car, etc.
d. making new things; a newly created machine
e. using knowledge or science to do things

SCAN
A. Guess the answer. Circle *a* or *b*.

How tall was the first skyscraper?

a. 10 stories   *b.* 50 stories

B. Scan the passage quickly to check your answer.

Building Skyscrapers

One hundred and fifty years ago, builders made **walls** from stone or **brick** with **iron** supports. These walls couldn't **support** very tall buildings. Then, builders started to **construct** buildings with **steel**. Steel is stronger and lighter than iron. It can support
5   very tall buildings.

The first building to have a **passenger** elevator was a five-story store in New York. The **invention** of the elevator made it possible to have much taller buildings. People didn't have to walk up hundreds of stairs to reach the top of the building.

10 People built the first skyscraper in Chicago in 1885. It was only 10 stories <u>high</u>. Now we build skyscrapers that are much, much taller. Two of the tallest are the Taipei 101 Tower in Taiwan and the Petronas Towers in Kuala Lumpur. Because of new **technology**, we now have stronger construction **materials** and faster elevators.
15 Skyscrapers will get taller and taller.

WHICH MEANING?
What does *high* mean in line 11?

1 (*adjective*) important
2 (*adjective*) tall
3 (*adjective*) a lot

CHECK YOUR COMPREHENSION

Read the passage again and answer the questions. Circle your answers.

MAIN IDEA

1. What is the main topic of this passage?

A. The first skyscraper
B. Skyscraper construction
C. The first elevator
D. The tallest buildings in the world

DETAIL

2. What did people use to construct buildings 150 years ago?

A. Stone
B. Brick
C. Iron
D. All of the above

3. What is true about the first passenger elevator?

A. It was in a five-story building.
B. It was built in 1885.
C. It was very fast.
D. It was in an office building.

4. Where was the first skyscraper?

A. New York
B. Chicago
C. Taiwan
D. Kuala Lumpur

INFERENCE

5. One hundred and fifty years ago, buildings

A. had steel supports.
B. weren't very tall.
C. had fast elevators.
D. didn't have stairs.

TEXT REFERENCE

6. In line 4, *It can support very tall buildings*, what does the word *It* refer to?

A. A wall
B. Iron
C. A builder
D. Steel

VOCABULARY REVIEW

MYSTERY PHRASE

Fill in the blanks to complete the sentences. Then use the letters in the circles to fill out the mystery phrase below. Hint: The circles are in the correct order.

1. You can see good views from the (◯) b s ☐ ☐ v ☐ t ☐ ☐ n area.

2. Take ☐ (◯) ☐ your shoes. The floor is clean.

3. Climbing towers is Alain Robert's (◯) ☐ b b ☐ .

4. Take an (◯) l ☐ v a ☐ ☐ r or climb up the stairs.

5. The elevator was an important (◯) n v ☐ ☐ ☐ o n .

6. Many p ☐ ☐ s e n (◯) ☐ r s ride these elevators every day.

7. He exercises at a (◯) ☐ a l ☐ ☐ club after school.

8. The test has two s e ☐ (◯) ☐ o n ☐ : listening and reading.

9. They used brick, steel, and other ☐ a t e ☐ ☐ a l (◯) to build the skyscraper.

Mystery phrase:

People who are afraid (◯)(◯) (◯)(◯)(◯)(◯)(◯)(◯) don't like skyscrapers.

WORDS IN CONTEXT

Fill in the blanks with words from each box.

permission	views	design	support	underground

1. I'll ask my parents for _____ to go to the party.

2. You don't have to park your car on the street. There is a big parking area _____.

3. These walls are strong. They can _____ a tall building.

4. Let's go to the top of the building. We can see good _____ from there.

5. The new building has an interesting _____. It looks like a big ship.

jail	elevators	technology	materials	take off

6. This building has fast _____. We can get to the top very quickly.

7. That woman stole money, and the police took her to _____.

8. _____ your sweater. It's very warm in here.

9. You need strong _____ to build a skyscraper.

10. _____ helps us do many things quickly and easily.

steel	stories	bamboo	brick	passengers

11. Some houses are made of wood, and some houses are made of _____.

12. This building isn't very tall. It only has four _____.

13. The elevator was very crowded. There were a lot of _____ on it.

14. People use _____ to build skyscrapers because it is so strong and light.

15. _____ is a beautiful plant. It looks very nice in a garden.

WORD FAMILIES

Fill in the blanks with words from each box.

usual (*adjective*)	unusual (*adjective*)	usually (*adverb*)

1. I _____ take the bus to school.

2. A cold day is _____ in the summer.

invention (*noun*)	inventor (*noun*)	invented (*verb*)

3. An _____ has to have a good imagination.

4. People _____ cars more than 100 years ago.

building (*noun*)	builder (*noun*)	build (*verb*)

5. My father works in a very tall _____.

6. They are going to _____ several new skyscrapers in our city.

WRONG WORD

One word in each group does not fit. Circle the word.

1. big	short	high	tall
2. house	skyscraper	building	park
3. paper	steel	iron	brick
4. wall	door	grass	window
5. store	salesman	school	shopping mall
6. construct	build	make	visit
7. bamboo	bird	tree	flower
8. concerned	happy	worried	afraid

SENTENCE COMPLETION
Complete the advertisement with words from the box.

concerned	floors	health club	shopping mall	underground

Do you like to shop? Then visit the city's new _____.

It's the biggest one in the city!

We have 150 stores on five _____.

Shop in our stores, eat in our fine restaurants, and exercise in our _____.

Are you _____ about parking? Don't worry! We have parking for 1,000 cars _____.

Visit us soon!

WHAT ABOUT YOU?
Speaking
Ask your partner these questions.

1. How many stories does your house or apartment building have?

2. What materials is your house made of?

3. What are your hobbies?

4. Which shopping malls do you like to visit?

5. What do you like to get when you go to a shopping mall?

Writing
Now write about your partner. Use your partner's answers to the questions.
Example: <u>John's house has one story</u>.

1. _____

2. _____

3. _____

4. _____

5. _____

READING QUIZ

Read the passage and answer the questions. Circle your answers.

The Empire State Building is a famous skyscraper in New York City. It was completed in 1931. At that time, it was the tallest building in the world. Since then, people have constructed several taller buildings.

5 The Empire State Building is 102 stories high. It has 73 elevators. The fastest ones travel more than 450 meters a minute. They can carry passengers to the 80th floor in 45 seconds.

The building is filled with offices. Many people work there, but nobody lives there. But, many people visit the building. They like
10 to go to the observation areas on the 86th and 102nd floors. They can enjoy good views of the city from there.

MAIN IDEA

1. What is the main topic of this passage?

A. The fastest elevators in the world

B. A skyscraper in New York

C. Visitors to New York

D. Working in the Empire State Building

DETAIL

2. How many elevators does the Empire State Building have?

A. 73

B. 80

C. 102

D. 450

3. What is true about the Empire State Building?

A. It is still the tallest building in the world.

B. It has 102 stories.

C. Many people live there.

D. Few people visit it.

TEXT REFERENCE

4. In line 6, *The fastest ones travel more than*, what does the word *ones* refer to?

A. Passengers

B. People

C. Elevators

D. Buildings

VOCABULARY

5. What does *constructed* in line 3 mean?

A. Wanted

B. Planned

C. Visited

D. Built

6. What does *observation* in line 10 mean?

A. Looking

B. Working

C. Talking

D. Visiting

ANTARCTICA

PEOPLE

Shackleton's ship the *Endurance*

PREPARE TO READ
Discuss these questions.

1. Look at the ship in the picture. Where in the world is it?

2. How do people travel in Antarctica? What do they eat?

WORD FOCUS
Match the words with their definitions.

A.

1. wages __   **a.** catch
2. darkness __   **b.** not sure; not probable
3. doubtful __   **c.** money you get for working; salary
4. sail __   **d.** no light
5. trap __   **e.** travel on a ship

B.

1. journey __   **a.** very windy and rainy or snowy
2. destroy __   **b.** made of wood
3. stormy __   **c.** break completely
4. rescue __   **d.** a trip
5. wooden __   **e.** remove from danger

SCAN
A. Guess the answer. Circle *a* or *b*.

Ernest Shackleton's ship was made of

a. steel.   *b.* wood.

B. Scan the passage quickly to check your answer.

ERNEST SHACKLETON

In 1914, Ernest Shackleton was looking for people to go with him on a **journey** to Antarctica. "Men wanted for dangerous journey. Small **wages**. Very cold. Long months of **darkness**. Safe return **doubtful**." He found 27 people. In December, they **sailed** for Antarctica on a ship
5   called the *Endurance*.

In Antarctica, thousands of miles from home, their **wooden** ship became **trapped** in the ice. They stayed with their ship for ten months <u>through</u> the cold, dark winter. Finally, the ice **destroyed** it.

The men had to walk for five months to reach open water. They pulled
10   three small boats with them. Shackleton and five others sailed in one of the small boats to find help. They sailed 800 miles and 17 days across **stormy** seas to reach South Georgia Island.

105 days later, the men whom Shackleton had left behind on the ice saw a ship. It was Shackleton coming back to **rescue** them. In August,
15   1916, all 28 returned home safely.

WHICH MEANING?
What does *through* mean in line 7?

1 (*adjective*) finished
2 (*preposition*) because of
3 (*preposition*) during

CHECK YOUR COMPREHENSION

Read the passage again and answer the questions. Circle your answers.

MAIN IDEA

1. What is the main topic of this passage?

A. A dangerous journey
B. Antarctica
C. The life of Ernest Shackleton
D. Sailing small boats

DETAIL

2. How many men went to Antarctica with Shackleton?

A. 14
B. 17
C. 27
D. 28

3. When did they begin their trip?

A. In August
B. In December
C. In 1916
D. In 1941

4. What was wrong with the ship?

A. The ice broke it.
B. It wasn't warm enough.
C. It didn't sail very fast.
D. There wasn't enough room for all the men.

5. What did the men do for five months?

A. They traveled home.
B. They waited on the ship.
C. They sailed in three small boats.
D. They walked across the ice.

INFERENCE

6. What is true about the men who sailed on the *Endurance*?

A. They didn't earn much money.
B. Some of them died on the ice.
C. Most of them were afraid of danger.
D. None of the above

PLACES

PREPARE TO READ
Discuss these questions.

1. Would you like to visit Antarctica?
Why or why not?

2. If you visit Antarctica, what will you see?

WORD FOCUS
Match the words with their definitions.

A.

1. blow __   **a.** a view of the land
2. cover __   **b.** go from one side to another
3. cross __   **c.** the action of the wind
4. landscape __   **d.** be on top of
5. penguin __   **e.** a type of bird that doesn't fly

B.

1. scientist __   **a.** a small animal that lives in the ground
2. seal __   **b.** a person on vacation
3. skis __   **c.** a type of sea animal
4. tourist __   **d.** a person who studies science
5. worm __   **e.** pieces of wood for the feet for going over snow

SCAN
A. Guess if this is true or false. Circle *a* or *b*.

There are trees in Antarctica.

a. True   *b*. False

B. Scan the passage quickly to check your answer.

Antarctica

Antarctica is the coldest place on Earth. Ice **covers** more than 99% of the continent. It also covers a lot of the sea around it. Of course, there is snow everywhere, too. It doesn't snow very often, but the wind always **blows** snow around.

5 There are no trees in Antarctica, and there are very few green plants. Tiny insects and **worms** are the only <u>land</u> animals. The sea has lots of different animals. There are different species of whales, **seals**, fish, and birds. The most famous birds are the **penguins**.

10 It is very difficult to live there, but people like to visit Antarctica. **Tourists** like to see the unusual **landscape** and the interesting animals. Climbers go to Mount Vinson, which is one of the Seven Summits. Other people **cross** the ice on foot or on **skis** to reach the South Pole. **Scientists** research the weather, plants,
15 and animals. Anyone who goes there has to love the cold.

WHICH MEANING?
What does *land* mean in line 6?
1 (*verb*) arrive
2 (*noun*) ground, not water
3 (*verb*) catch

CHECK YOUR COMPREHENSION

Read the passage again and answer the questions. Circle your answers.

MAIN IDEA

1. What is the main topic of this passage?

A. Interesting sea animals
B. Scientists in Antarctica
C. A cold continent
D. Mount Vinson

DETAIL

2. What is Antarctica?

A. A piece of ice
B. A continent
C. An island
D. A mountain

3. What can you see on the land in Anarctica?

A. Many green plants
B. Sand
C. Water
D. Snow and ice

4. Which of these animals live in the sea around Antarctica?

A. Birds
B. Worms
C. Insects
D. Snakes

INFERENCE

5. What is something that scientists can study in Antarctica?

A. Large land animals
B. Many different kinds of green plants
C. Animals that live in cold weather
D. Rainy weather

TEXT REFERENCE

6. In line 2, *It also covers a lot of the sea*, what does the word *It* refer to?

A. Snow
B. Ice
C. Continent
D. Antarctica

THINGS

emperor penguins

PREPARE TO READ
Discuss these questions.

1. What do you know about penguins?

2. How are penguins different from other birds?

WORD FOCUS
Match the words with their definitions.

A.
1. female __   **a.** a baby bird comes out of its egg
2. side by side __   **b.** man
3. hatch __   **c.** woman
4. lay __   **d.** next to each other
5. male __   **e.** a mother bird puts an egg in the nest

B.
1. freeze __   **a.** be on your feet
2. stand __   **b.** become very cold; become ice
3. survive __   **c.** be on or next to something
4. touch __   **d.** baby animal(s)
5. young __   **e.** live through something difficult

SCAN
A. Guess the answer. Circle _a_ or _b_.

How do emperor penguins make their nests?

a. They use branches and leaves.   *b.* They use their feet.

B. Scan the passage quickly to check your answer.

Emperor Penguins

Most species of birds have nests of branches and leaves, but emperor penguins don't. They use their feet for a nest.

A **female** emperor penguin **lays** one egg in May or June. She then goes away to sea to look for food. She leaves the male to take care of the egg. The **male**
5 penguin holds the egg on his feet to keep it warm. If the egg **touches** the ice, it will **freeze** and die.

June is the middle of winter in Antarctica. It is dark and windy. Everything is frozen. Male penguins stand **side by side** in large groups to keep each other warm. They **stand** like this for four months until the eggs **hatch**.

10 When the eggs hatch, the female penguins <u>return</u>. Together, the parents take care of the **young**. By summer, the young are bigger and can look for food by themselves. By winter, they are big enough to **survive** the cold without their parents.

WHICH MEANING?
What does *return* mean in line 10?
1 (*verb*) go back to a place
2 (*noun*) money that you earn
3 (*verb*) give something back to its owner

CHECK YOUR COMPREHENSION

Read the passage again and answer the questions. Circle your answers.

MAIN IDEA
1. What is the main topic of this passage?
   A. How birds survive the winter in Antarctica
   B. The life of a female penguin
   C. How emperor penguins take care of their eggs and babies
   D. The seasons in Antarctica

DETAIL
2. How many eggs does a female emperor penguin lay?
   A. None
   B. One
   C. Two
   D. Many

3. What do the female penguins do after they lay their eggs?
   A. They take care of the eggs.
   B. They look for food.
   C. They make nests.
   D. They eat the eggs.

4. How do the male penguins stay warm all winter?
   A. They stand next to each other in groups.
   B. They sit on their nests.
   C. They stand on their eggs.
   D. They sit with the female penguins.

INFERENCE
5. When do emperor penguins lay their eggs?
   A. In the spring
   B. In the summer
   C. In the fall
   D. In the winter

TEXT REFERENCE
6. In line 12, *By winter, they are big enough to survive the cold without their parents*, what does the word *they* refer to?
   A. Male penguins
   B. Female penguins
   C. Penguins' eggs
   D. Baby penguins

VOCABULARY REVIEW

WORD SEARCH
Find and circle the vocabulary below.

blow	
cross	
doubtful	
hatch	
journey	
landscape	
penguins	
rescue	
scientists	
trap	

```
U  Q  D  S  H  A  T  C  H  L  H  B  O  Y  L
Q  A  W  C  H  E  H  F  S  S  M  P  L  E  C
G  H  H  I  Z  C  N  L  B  H  Z  A  G  N  G
A  U  X  E  F  Q  W  G  T  O  N  S  J  R  Z
R  J  N  F  Y  U  N  N  D  B  G  I  U  Z
L  U  F  T  B  U  O  D  S  L  E  J  I  O  J
C  K  H  I  S  O  Q  C  O  U  R  B  Y  J  C
C  A  F  S  K  N  A  W  C  E  P  D  Q  M  Z
J  R  Z  T  L  P  I  S  D  A  W  O  W  U  B
W  L  O  S  E  V  E  U  O  N  J  F  B  F  Z
N  C  P  S  R  P  H  G  F  P  G  R  T  C
Z  E  W  V  S  D  D  D  X  N  M  N  W  R  M
T  B  H  D  E  Z  L  D  Z  D  E  I  U  A  N
N  K  Y  A  E  H  D  D  A  R  O  P  J  P  F
Q  K  A  S  W  S  G  Y  R  A  I  W  S  T  G
```

WORDS IN CONTEXT
Fill in the blanks with words from each box.

return	stand	through	wages	touch

1. We stayed at the beach _____ the summer.
2. Don't _____ that plate! It's very hot.
3. The _____ for this job are $400 a week.
4. You'll probably get tired if you _____ for a long time.
5. They went on vacation. They'll _____ next week.

cross	young	tourists	side by side	covers

6. The sea _____ most of the Earth.
7. Emperor penguins stand _____ all winter. When they are next to each other, they stay warm.
8. Many _____ visit Antarctica. There are interesting things to see there.
9. Animals teach their _____ to find food.
10. It's dangerous to _____ the sea in a small boat.

journey	seals	hatch	freezes	land

11. They went on a long _____ to Antarctica. They traveled for two years.

12. Snow and ice cover most of the _____ in Antarctica.

13. _____ are interesting animals that like to play and swim in cold water.

14. There are eggs in that nest. Soon they'll _____, and we'll see the young birds.

15. That lake _____ when the weather is very cold.

WORD FAMILIES
Fill in the blanks with words from each box.

survival (*noun*)	**survivor** (*noun*)	**survive** (*verb*)

1. In cold places, _____ is very difficult.

2. Baby animals cannot _____ without their parents.

destruction (*noun*)	**destroy** (*verb*)	**destructive** (*adjective*)

3. Strong winds are very _____.

4. Storms can _____ trees and buildings.

science (*noun*)	**scientist** (*noun*)	**scientific** (*adjective*)

5. _____ research in Antarctica has taught us a lot about the weather.

6. _____ is a very interesting subject to study.

TRUE OR FALSE?
Are the following sentences true or false? Circle your answers.

1. Water freezes in warm weather.	TRUE	FALSE
2. Male emperor penguins build nests.	TRUE	FALSE
3. Female penguins lay eggs.	TRUE	FALSE
4. Seals live in the sea.	TRUE	FALSE
5. Worms are very large animals.	TRUE	FALSE
6. You can go down a mountain on skis.	TRUE	FALSE
7. Whales are land animals.	TRUE	FALSE
8. It's easy to see in darkness.	TRUE	FALSE

SENTENCE COMPLETION
Complete the letter with words from the box.

young	stormy	tourists	blowing	skis

Dear Mom and Dad,

I am thrilled to be in Antarctica. The weather is very _____ right now, and the wind is _____ hard. We hope the weather will be better tomorrow because we plan to cross the snow on _____. We saw some penguins yesterday with their _____. The baby penguins were so little and cute. Many people visit Antarctica at this time of year. There are a lot of _____ here now. I am having a great time.

Love,

Tom

WHAT ABOUT YOU?
Speaking
Ask your partner these questions.

1. Would you prefer to sail or ski? Why?

2. What do you do when the weather is stormy?

3. What can you see in the landscape around your home?

4. To what place would you like to take a journey?

5. What time do you usually return home every day?

Writing
Now write about your partner. Use your partner's answers to the questions.
Example: <u>Barbara would prefer to sail because she loves the sea</u>.

1. _____

2. _____

3. _____

4. _____

5. _____

READING QUIZ

Read the passage and answer the questions. Circle your answers.

Roald Amundsen wanted to be the first person to reach the South Pole. Other people were planning journeys to the South Pole, too. So, Amundsen didn't tell anybody about his plan. At first, he didn't even tell the men who went with
5　him. He told them when they were on the ship sailing to Antarctica.

Amundsen and his group reached Antarctica in January, 1911. Then, they spent several months preparing for their journey. Finally on October 19, Amundsen and four other
10　men left for the South Pole. The darkness of winter was over, but the weather was still cold. They traveled through good weather and stormy weather. The wind blew often as they crossed the frozen landscape on their skis, but they continued their journey. They traveled for weeks. On
15　December 14, 1911, they finally reached the South Pole. They were the first to do it.

MAIN IDEA

1. What is the main topic of this passage?

　A. Skiing in Antarctica
　B. The first trip to the South Pole
　C. The weather in Antarctica
　D. A famous ship

DETAIL

2. When did Amundsen reach Antarctica?

　A. January
　B. September
　C. October
　D. December

3. How did Amundsen travel across Antarctica to the South Pole?

　A. By ship
　B. By car
　C. On foot
　D. On skis

VOCABULARY

4. What does *journey* in line 9 mean?

　A. Trip
　B. Vacation
　C. Research
　D. Exercise

5. What does *frozen* in line 13 mean?

　A. White
　B. Open
　C. Cold
　D. Dark

TEXT REFERENCE

6. In line 16, *They were the first to do it*, what does the word *it* refer to?

　A. Travel on skis
　B. Sail to Antarctica
　C. Reach the South Pole
　D. Travel in stormy weather

Midori Ito

THE OLYMPICS

PEOPLE

PREPARE TO READ
Discuss these questions.

1. What is your favorite winter sport? Why do you like it?

2. Do you know any other famous ice skaters? Who are they?

WORD FOCUS
Match the words with their definitions.

A.
1. amazing __   **a.** winner
2. apologize __   **b.** say "sorry"
3. champion __   **c.** sports event
4. chance __   **d.** wonderful
5. competition __ **e.** possibility; opportunity

B.
1. performance __ **a.** a sport on ice
2. jump __   **b.** very good at doing something
3. medal __   **c.** pushing yourself up with your legs
4. skating __   **d.** something you do for people to see
5. skillful __   **e.** a metal prize: gold, silver, or bronze

SCAN
A. Guess the answer. Circle *a* or *b*.

Where is Midori Ito from?

a. The United States   *b.* Japan

B. Scan the passage quickly to check your answer.

Midori Ito

Midori Ito, the Japanese **skating champion**, wanted to win a gold **medal** at the 1992 Olympics. She was a very **skillful** skater, and she was famous for her **amazing jumps**. In 1989, she skated in the World Championships in Paris. In that **competition**, she
5 did a very difficult jump. She became the first Asian skater to win this competition.

At the 1992 Olympics, she skated and did some very <u>hard</u> jumps, but she fell twice. She thought she had lost her **chance** at a medal, but her other skillful jumps helped her. She won the
10 silver medal for her **performance**. But, it wasn't a gold medal. She **apologized** to her country because she didn't win the gold.

After the 1992 Olympic Games, Ito continued to skate, but not in competitions. She did return to the Olympics, but not as a skater. She worked for Japanese television in both the 1998 and
15 2002 Winter Olympic Games.

WHICH MEANING?
What does *hard* mean in line 7?

1 (*adjective*) not soft
2 (*adjective*) not easy
3 (*adjective*) not nice

CHECK YOUR COMPREHENSION

Read the passage again and answer the questions. Circle your answers.

MAIN IDEA

1. What is the main topic of this passage?

A. The sport of skating
B. The Winter Olympic Games
C. A champion skater
D. A gold medal

DETAIL

2. When did Ito skate in the Olympics?

A. 1989
B. 1992
C. 1998
D. 2002

3. What did Ito do in Paris?

A. She won a competition.
B. She fell.
C. She did an easy jump.
D. She worked for Japanese television.

4. Why did Ito apologize to her country?

A. She didn't get the best medal.
B. She didn't jump skillfully.
C. She lost her chance at a medal.
D. She hurt herself in the competition.

5. What did Ito do after the 1992 Olympics?

A. She skated in the World Championships.
B. She became an actress.
C. She stopped skating in competitions.
D. She bought a television.

INFERENCE

6. How did Ito feel when she didn't win an Olympic gold medal?

A. Proud
B. Sorry
C. Lucky
D. Angry

ATHENS 2004

PREPARE TO READ
Discuss these questions.

1. Where were the first Olympic Games? When did they take place?

2. In what other cities did the Olympics take place?

WORD FOCUS
Match the words with their definitions.

A.

1. athlete __   **a.** new; not ancient
2. modern __   **b.** happen
3. stadium __   **c.** a place for sports events
4. take place __   **d.** a stick with fire on top
5. torch __   **e.** a person who is good at sports

B.

1. runner __   **a.** form
2. remind __   **b.** middle; important part
3. shape __   **c.** make someone remember
4. enter __   **d.** a person who runs
5. center __   **e.** go in

SCAN
A. Guess the answer. Circle *a* or *b*.

When did the Olympics begin?

a. 1,200 years ago   *b.* 2,700 years ago

B. Scan the passage quickly to check your answer.

GREECE AND THE OLYMPICS

Greece was the home of the very first Olympic Games. The Games began almost 2,700 years ago in Olympia, Greece. They **took place** every four years, like today. These ancient games lasted for about 1,200 years.

The Olympic Games started again in 1896. The ancient games were competitions
5 between Greek cities. The **modern** Olympics are competitions between countries.

The first modern Olympics took place in the Panathenaic **Stadium** in Athens. Builders constructed the new stadium for the 1896 Olympics in the **shape** of the letter U, just like the ancient stadium.

Greece is still the **center** of the Olympics. People <u>light</u> the Olympic **torch** in
10 Olympia, Greece. Then, **runners** carry it across the world to reach the city where the games will take place. When the Olympic Games open, the Greek **athletes** always **enter** the stadium first. This is to **remind** everyone of the country where the Olympics began.

> **WHICH MEANING?**
> **What does *light* mean in line 9?**
> **1** (*noun*) lamp
> **2** (*adjective*) not heavy
> **3** (*verb*) start a fire

CHECK YOUR COMPREHENSION

Read the passage again and answer the questions. Circle your answers.

MAIN IDEA

1. What is this passage mainly about?

  A. A stadium in Athens

  B. The Olympic torch

  C. Greek athletes

  D. The place where the Olympics began

DETAIL

2. What is true about the ancient Olympic Games?

  A. They were competitions between countries.

  B. They took place every four years.

  C. They lasted for only a few years.

  D. They took place in Athens.

3. When did the modern Olympics begin?

  A. In 1200

  B. In 1700

  C. In 1896

  D. In 1986

4. At the Olympic Games, who enters the stadium first?

  A. The runners

  B. The Greek athletes

  C. The stadium builders

  D. The torch holders

INFERENCE

5. Why did the first modern Olympic Games take place in Greece?

  A. To remember the ancient Olympic Games

  B. Because there was a new stadium there

  C. To help the tourist business in Athens

  D. Because Greek athletes are the best

TEXT REFERENCE

6. In line 10, *Then, runners carry it across the world*, what does the word *it* refer to?

  A. A flag

  B. A map

  C. A torch

  D. A key

THINGS

PREPARE TO READ
Discuss these questions.

1. Which sports were part of the ancient Olympic Games?

2. What are some modern summer and winter Olympic sports?

WORD FOCUS
Match the words with their definitions.

A.
1. boxing ___   **a.** a sport played with a stick, on ice
2. distance ___   **b.** a sport involving jumps, balance, and strength
3. exercise ___   **c.** length; how far something is
4. gymnastics ___   **d.** a fighting sport
5. hockey ___   **e.** activities to make your body stronger

B.
1. participate ___   **a.** a competition with horses
2. skiing ___   **b.** riding a bicycle
3. swimming ___   **c.** a sport in the water
4. bicycling ___   **d.** be part of an activity
5. horse racing ___   **e.** a sport done in snowy mountains

SCAN
A. Guess the answer. Circle *a* or *b*.

Which sport took place at the first Olympics in ancient Greece?

a. Running   *b.* Bicycling

B. Scan the passage quickly to check your answer.

Olympic Sports

The first Olympics in ancient Greece lasted one day. There was only one sport—running. The athletes ran a **distance** of 192.27 meters. Later, the games included more sports, like **boxing** and **horse racing**. Unlike modern athletes, the athletes in the ancient Olympics didn't
5　have special sports clothes. In fact, they didn't wear any clothes at all.

Like the ancient Olympics, the first modern Olympics in 1896 included running. It had more modern sports, too. These included **swimming**, **gymnastics**, and **bicycling**. The organizers felt that sports and **exercise** made people better human beings. This <u>time</u>, the athletes wore clothes.

10　The Olympics in ancient Greece didn't include winter sports. The first winter Olympics took place in France in 1924. The sports included **skiing**, skating, and **hockey**.

Women didn't **participate** in the ancient Olympics. Women didn't participate in the first modern Olympic Games, either, but that soon
15　changed. In the 1900 Olympics, women participated in several sports.

WHICH MEANING?
What does *time* mean in line 9?

1 (*noun*) minutes and hours
2 (*noun*) occasion; event
3 (*verb*) count minutes and hours

CHECK YOUR COMPREHENSION

Read the passage again and answer the questions. Circle your answers.

MAIN IDEA

1. What is this passage mainly about?

   A. The most popular Olympic sports
   B. The history of Olympic sports
   C. Olympic athletes
   D. Olympic clothes

DETAIL

2. How long did the first Olympics in ancient Greece last?

   A. One day
   B. Several days
   C. 27 days
   D. 192 days

3. What is true about the first Olympics in ancient Greece?

   A. The athletes wore special clothes.
   B. The runners ran 197 meters.
   C. There was only one sport.
   D. Women participated in several sports.

4. When did women first participate in the modern Olympics?

   A. 1896
   B. 1900
   C. 1924
   D. 1942

5. Which of the following was NOT played at the 1924 winter Olympics?

   A. Skiing
   B. Hockey
   C. Snowboarding
   D. Skating

INFERENCE

6. What is true about the first modern Olympics?

   A. The only sport was running.
   B. There were no winter sports.
   C. Gymnastics was the most popular sport.
   D. None of the above

VOCABULARY REVIEW

CROSSWORD PUZZLE

Complete the crossword using the clues.

Across

2. Something that makes you say "Wow!" is _____.

5. You can win a gold, silver, or bronze one.

6. go in

7. to say you are sorry

8. a stick of fire that Olympic athletes carry

Down

1. a sport between two fighters

3. opposite of ancient

4. a sport that involves jumping, balance, and strength

WORDS IN CONTEXT

Fill in the blanks with words from each box.

horse racing	stadium	champion	remind	swimming

1. There's a big soccer _____ in my city. I've seen several games there.

2. There's a pool in the park near my house. I go _____ there on weekends.

3. Please _____ me to call Sam tomorrow. I don't want to forget.

4. It's fun to watch _____. It's fun to see the horses go fast.

5. Midori Ito is a _____ skater. She has won a lot of competitions.

light	chance	times	bicycling	skating

6. I love _____. I ride every weekend.

7. It's dark in here. We need to _____ a candle.

8. The best athletes have the _____ to go to the Olympics.

9. I have watched the Olympics many _____.

10. I love _____. I like to be on the ice.

skiing	medal	shape	enter	distance

11. The _____ of this stadium is round.

12. The runners ran a long _____. They got very tired.

13. We can _____ the stadium through this door.

14. We went _____ in the mountains last weekend.

15. Jim was the fastest runner. He won a gold _____.

WORD FAMILIES
Fill in the blanks with words from each box.

skills (*noun*)	**skillful** (*adjective*)	**skillfully** (*adverb*)

1. Olympic athletes have to have a lot of _____.

2. Mary won a medal because she skated very _____.

competition (*noun*)	**competes** (*verb*)	**competitive** (*adjective*)

3. Some people are very _____. They want to win at everything.

4. John _____ in several sports.

performance (*noun*)	**performer** (*noun*)	**perform** (*verb*)

5. Olympic athletes _____ in front of thousands of people.

6. He practices every day, so his _____ will be perfect.

SYNONYMS
Circle the word in each group that is nearest in meaning to the word in bold.

1. hard	boring	difficult	long	broken
2. modern	nice	pretty	clean	new
3. competition	game	talking	swimming	action
4. take place	sit down	remove	happen	leave
5. center	end	middle	place	start

TRUE OR FALSE?
Are the following sentences true or false? Circle your answers.

1. You need snow to play hockey.	TRUE	FALSE
2. Runners move slowly.	TRUE	FALSE
3. Skiing is a winter sport.	TRUE	FALSE
4. The Olympics take place every three years.	TRUE	FALSE
5. Olympic skaters have to jump well.	TRUE	FALSE
6. Only men participate in the Olympics.	TRUE	FALSE
7. Gymnastics is an outdoor sport.	TRUE	FALSE

WHAT ABOUT YOU?
Speaking
Ask your partner these questions.

1. Where do you go to get exercise?

2. Which sports do you participate in?

3. Who is your favorite athlete?

4. What is a hard thing that you have done?

5. How do you remind yourself to do important things?

Writing
Now write about your partner. Use your partner's answers to the questions.

Example: <u>Dave goes to the park to get exercise.</u>

1. _____

2. _____

3. _____

4. _____

5. _____

READING QUIZ

Read the passage and answer the questions. Circle your answers.

Dear Sports Man,

I love skating. Someday, I want to be a skating champion. How can I reach my goal?

Skating Sam

5 Dear Sam,

Skating is a great sport. It's also hard. If you want to be a good skater, you have to practice every day. You have to learn how to do difficult jumps. You also have to do exercises to be strong. A good skating teacher can help
10 you with all these things.

When you are ready, you can participate in competitions. If you perform well, you can win a medal. But don't worry if you don't get one the first time. You'll always have another chance. Most skating champions practice
15 for years before they win medals. It's important to work hard and do your best, but don't forget to have fun, too.

Sports Man

MAIN IDEA

1. Why did Sam write the letter?

A. He wants to become a skating teacher.

B. He wants to watch a skating competition.

C. He wants help to become a skating champion.

D. He wants to buy better skates.

DETAIL

2. How can someone become a better skater?

A. Practice every day.

B. Learn jumps.

C. Do exercises.

D. All of the above

3. What is true about skating champions?

A. They usually win medals the first time.

B. They never have fun.

C. They practice for a long time.

D. They always perform well.

TEXT REFERENCE

4. In line 13, *But don't worry if you don't get one the first time*, what does the word *one* refer to?

A. A teacher

B. A medal

C. A competition

D. A chance

VOCABULARY

5. What does *medal* in line 12 mean?

A. Money

B. Game

C. Prize

D. Toy

6. What does *perform* in line 12 mean?

A. Do

B. Learn

C. Teach

D. Watch

VOCABULARY SELF-QUIZ

You can use these word lists to quiz yourself.

1. First, write your translations next to the English words. Study them for a while.

2. Then, quiz yourself. Cover up the English words. You should only look at your translations.

3. Try to remember the English words and write them down. How many words can you remember?

Unit 1

PEOPLE	TRANSLATION	TEST YOURSELF
author		
continue		
famous		
graduation		
grow up		
make up		
passion		
publisher		
rabbit		
write down		

PLACES		
attend		
broom		
castle		
invisible		
magic		
monster		
ordinary		
recess		
witch		
wizard		

THINGS		
available		
characters		
costumes		
event		
imagine		
million		
products		
put on		
series		
Website		

Unit 2

PEOPLE	TRANSLATION	TEST YOURSELF
communicate		
feel		
fireworks		
gorilla		
human		
nickname		
psychology		
research		
sign language		
zoo		

PLACES		
branches		
cut down		
endangered		
insects		
jungle		
nest		
plant		
safe		
species		
the wild		

THINGS		
doll		
favorite		
ill		
pain		
set free		
sign		
terrible		
tofu		
toothache		
whale		

Unit 3

PEOPLE	TRANSLATION	TEST YOURSELF
blind		
climb		
despite		
disabilities		
especially		
fail		
proud		
reach		
summit		
wheelchair		

PLACES		
achievement		
adventure		
challenge		
continent		
Earth		
extra		
goal		
peak		
pole		
record		

THINGS		
energy		
ground		
oxygen		
pick up		
pile		
rip		
several		
take away		
tents		
trash		

Unit 4

PEOPLE	TRANSLATION	TEST YOURSELF
clue		
create		
crime		
detective		
escape		
fans		
mystery		
popular		
single		
solve		

PLACES

ancient		
builder		
calendar		
heavy		
nature		
purpose		
religious		
season		
shadow		
stone		

THINGS

arrest		
correct		
everywhere		
guess		
lucky		
missing		
psychic		
relative		
search		
woods		

Unit 5

PEOPLE	TRANSLATION	TEST YOURSELF
accident		
agent		
change (out of)		
fashion		
model		
spot		
suddenly		
thrilled		
uniform		
wealthiest		

PLACES		
active		
artistic		
casual		
express		
hang up		
mess		
organize		
personality		
practical		
take care of		

THINGS		
appearance		
common		
disagree		
equal		
obey		
rules		
tradition		
turn into		
unattractive		
uncomfortable		

Unit 6

PEOPLE	TRANSLATION	TEST YOURSELF
building		
concerned		
hobby		
jail		
permission		
salesman		
stories		
take off		
tower		
unusual		

PLACES		
bamboo		
design		
elevators		
health club		
observation		
section		
shopping mall		
skyscraper		
underground		
views		

THINGS		
brick		
construct		
invention		
iron		
materials		
passenger		
steel		
support		
technology		
wall		

Unit 7

PEOPLE	TRANSLATION	TEST YOURSELF
darkness		
destroy		
doubtful		
journey		
rescue		
sail		
stormy		
trap		
wages		
wooden		

PLACES		
blow		
cover		
cross		
landscape		
penguin		
scientist		
seal		
skis		
tourist		
worm		

THINGS		
female		
freeze		
hatch		
lay		
male		
side by side		
stand		
survive		
touch		
young		

Unit 8

PEOPLE	TRANSLATION	TEST YOURSELF
amazing		
apologize		
champion		
chance		
competition		
jump		
medal		
performance		
skating		
skillful		

PLACES		
athlete		
center		
enter		
modern		
remind		
runner		
shape		
stadium		
take place		
torch		

THINGS		
bicycling		
boxing		
distance		
exercise		
gymnastics		
hockey		
horse racing		
participate		
skiing		
swimming		

VOCABULARY INDEX

The numbers refer to the pages where the words appear in the reading passages.

COMMON IRREGULAR VERBS

INFINITIVE	SIMPLE PAST	PAST PARTICIPLE
be	was/were	been
become	became	become
begin	began	begun
blow	blew	blown
break	broke	broken
bring	brought	brought
build	built	built
buy	bought	bought
catch	caught	caught
choose	chose	chosen
come	came	come
cost	cost	cost
cut	cut	cut
do	did	done
draw	drew	drawn
drive	drove	driven
eat	ate	eaten
fall	fell	fallen
feel	felt	felt
find	found	found
fly	flew	flown
forget	forgot	forgotten
freeze	froze	frozen
get	got	gotten
give	gave	given
go	went	gone/been
grow	grew	grown
hang	hung	hung
have	had	had
hear	heard	heard
hold	held	held
hurt	hurt	hurt
keep	kept	kept
know	knew	known
lay	laid	laid
leave	left	left

INFINITIVE	SIMPLE PAST	PAST PARTICIPLE
let	let	let
light	lit/lighted	lit/lighted
lose	lost	lost
make	made	made
mean	meant	meant
meet	met	met
pay	paid	paid
put	put	put
read	read	read
ride	rode	ridden
ring	rang	rung
run	ran	run
say	said	said
see	saw	seen
sell	sold	sold
send	sent	sent
set	set	set
show	showed	shown
sing	sang	sung
sit	sat	sat
sleep	slept	slept
speak	spoke	spoken
spend	spent	spent
stand	stood	stood
steal	stole	stolen
swim	swam	swum
take	took	taken
teach	taught	taught
tear	tore	torn
tell	told	told
think	thought	thought
throw	threw	thrown
understand	understood	understood
wear	wore	worn
win	won	won
write	wrote	written